Cooking
— con —
Claudia

Cooking
— con —
Claudia

100 Authentic, Family-Style Mexican Recipes

Claudia Regalado

Publisher Mike Sanders
Editorial Director Ann Barton
Editor Brandon Buechley
Art & Design Director William Thomas
Copy Editor Christopher Stolle
Cover & Interior Design Studio Noel
Compositor Ayanna Lacey
Lifestyle Photography Melissa Valladares
Food Photography Daniel Showalter
Food Stylist & Recipe Tester Lovoni Walker
Chef Ashley Brooks
Senior Layout Technician Ayanna Lacey
Proofreaders Claire Safran, Lisa Himes
Indexer Celia McCoy

First American Edition, 2023
Published in the United States by DK Publishing
1745 Broadway, 20th Floor, New York, NY 10019

The authorized representative in the EEA is Dorling Kindersley
Verlag GmbH. Arnulfstr. 124, 80636 Munich, Germany

Copyright © 2023 by Claudia Regalado
25 26 27 10 9 8 7 6 5
005-336315-OCT2023

Library of Congress Catalog Number: 2023931552
ISBN 978-0-7440-8388-0

DK books are available at special discounts when purchased in bulk
for sales promotions, premiums, fund-raising, or educational use.
For details, contact: SpecialSales@dk.com

Printed and bound in China

www.dk.com

MIX
Paper | Supporting
responsible forestry
FSC™ C018179

This book was made with Forest
Stewardship Council ™ certified
paper - one small step in DK's
commitment to a sustainable future.
**For more information go to
www.dk.com/our-green-pledge**

To my supporters, thank you
for trusting me and allowing
me to be part of your family.
You'll forever be part of mine.

Contents

Welcome to My Kitchen 10

Introduction 12

The Journey to Cooking con Claudia 14

The Regalado Family 20

My Kitchen Essentials 22

Equipment 24

Ingredients 26

Roasting Steps & Techniques 31

Drinks 32

Agua Fresca de Pepino con Limón 34

Agua Fresca de Hibisco con Fresas 36

Agua Fresca de Piña Colada 38

Agua Fresca de Sandia y Pepino 40

Café de Olla Helado 42

Café de Olla 44

Horchata de Fresa 45

Horchata 46

Horchata de Chocolate 48

Atole de Galletas 50

Champurrado 52

Appetizers & Sides 54

Ensalada de Calabacita 56

Ceviche de Camarón 58

Coctel de Camarón 60

Ensalada de Pollo 62

Frijoles de la Olla 64

Arroz Blanco 65

Arroz Rojo 66

Espagueti Verde 68

Espagueti Rojo 70

Tortitas de Papa y Queso 72

Tortillas & Bread 74

Pan Bolillo 76

Concha 78

Masa Basica para Antojitos 80

Masa para Tamales 81

Donas Mexicanas 82

Tortillas de Harina 84

Tortillas de Maiz 86

Dips & Salsas 88

Guacamole 90

Pico de Gallo 92

Salsa Macha 94

Salsa Roja 96

Salsa Verde 98

Salsa de Aguacate 100

Chile con Queso Dip 101

Soups & Stews 102

Asado de Boda 104

Birria de Res 106

Caldo de Albóndigas 108

Caldo de Camarón 110

Caldo de Pollo con Arroz 112

Caldo de Res 114

Carne con Chiles y Papas 116

Sopa de Conchitas con Pollo 118

Chile Colorado 119

Chile Verde 120

Menudo 122

Pozole Verde de Pollo 124

Mole de Olla 126

Pozole Rojo 128

Sopa de Fideo con Carne 130

Sopa Azteca 132

Breakfast Entrees 134

Chilaquiles Rojos 136

Chilaquiles Verde 138

Burritos para el Desayuno 140

Huevos Encobijados 141

Huevos Rancheros 142

Huevos Ahogados 144

Beef Entrees 146

Barbacoa 148

Barbacoa de Res 150

Bistec Ranchero con Papas 152

Taquitos Dorados de Carne Molida 154

Tacos de Deshebrada 155

Carne Asada 156

Discada 158

Gorditas de Picadillo en Chile Verde ... 160

Chicken Entrees 162

Enchiladas Verdes con Pollo 164

Enmoladas con Pollo 166

Pollo Asado 168

Arroz con Pollo 170

Entomatadas con Pollo 171

Mole de Pollo 172

Tacos de Alambre 174

Taquitos Dorados de Pollo con Consommé 176

Tinga de Pollo 178

Tinga Verde de Pollo 180

Pork Entrees 182

Tacos al Pastor 184

Carnitas 186

Chilorio 188

Tamales Verdes 189

Tamales Rojos 190

Pambazos de Papas con Chorizo 192

Tacos de Canasta 194

Seafood, Veggie & Egg Entrees 196

Camarónes a la Diabla 198

Tacos de Camarón 200

Tacos Gobernador 202

Tacos de Pescado 204

Tamales de Rajas con Queso 205

Chile Rellenos 206

Enchiladas Rojas 208

Enfrijoladas 210

Migas a la Mexicana 212

Desserts 214

Arroz con Leche 216

Bionicos 218

Fresas con Crema 220

Gelatina de Mosaico 222

Gelatina Fresas con Crema 224

Churros 225

Buñuelos 226

Choco Flan 228

Pastel Tres Leches 230

Index 232

Acknowledgments 238

XO, Claudia 240

Welcome to My Kitchen

Hi guys, hello and welcome!

If you are new here, my name is Claudia. I have been a YouTube chef for five years and a home cook for more than fifteen years.

In this book, you are going to learn all about my super easy and delicious authentic Mexican recipes that were created right here in my kitchen. Most of my recipes have been passed down from generation to generation and have become favorites in not only my family but also many others—and I hope they become yours too! I want to be the motivation you need to get in the kitchen and learn all about Mexican cuisine and just how delicious it is. After all, cooking doesn't have to be complicated, and the most important thing to remember is to add the best ingredient of all—love.

Introduction

The Journey to Cooking con Claudia............................14

The Regalado-Mendoza Family.................................20

The Journey to Cooking con Claudia

I was born in 1991 in the state of Durango, Mexico. As crazy as it sounds, I remember my first five years of life in Mexico as if they were yesterday. I loved spending time with my grandmothers, including making tortillas and fetching eggs from the chickens. But this time didn't last long, as my parents made the biggest decision of their lives and decided to cross over to the United States illegally in hopes of a better life and future.

It took me a while to adapt to life in Arizona, where my family decided to settle. From food, culture, and school to celebrations, and most importantly, language, Mexico and the United States are two very different worlds. From kindergarten to third grade I was able to attend bilingual classes, which I loved because it still felt a little like home. However, after third grade, bilingual classes were no longer an option and my world took a turn. It took me an entire year to adapt to a new language at that age.

While I was experiencing my own struggles at school, my parents worked tirelessly to provide for me and my three brothers. I was the oldest child, but my childhood wasn't ordinary. I spent every summer taking care of my brothers while my parents worked. I didn't come back to school with stories of fun summer vacations and adventures like all my peers seemed to. My stories were of the dishes I cooked for my brothers to keep everyone happy and fed while my parents were away at work.

When I was fifteen, I became pregnant with my first child and I felt like I'd let my parents down. They'd worked so hard to provide a better life for us and I didn't want to disappoint them. At seventeen, I married my husband and our family continued to grow. I graduated high school and knew I needed to decide on the kind of future I wanted, especially so I could make sure my parents' hard work meant something at the end of the day. Having always been into hair and beauty, I initially decided to pursue a career in cosmetology, but after a move to Texas I pivoted and began pursuing a nursing career. Simply put, I always knew I wanted to help people in one way or another.

I enrolled in a college nursing program and received a nursing assistant certification after six weeks. I began working in a nursing home and quickly found so much joy in getting to help others, especially people who didn't have the

means to take care of themselves. After six months, we decided Texas didn't feel like home and moved back to Arizona. I found a new position as a nursing assistant in a facility as our family continued to grow. Honestly, we struggled quite a bit during this time, but we knew we could conquer anything as a family that stuck together. This was also the time when I was finally able to help my parents become legal citizens. Their days of worrying were at an end and I'll forever be so proud of and grateful for this accomplishment.

When I was twenty-three, my husband and I bought our first house! We had four kids at this point (with another on the way), but we were finally thriving. We had many goals, including my going back to school to complete my nursing degree, but God had different plans. I continued with two more years of college before one of my classes required I film a video about myself and upload it to YouTube. I've always been a very shy person and not the best talker. Reluctantly, I produced my video and uploaded it—and started getting subscribers!

At that time, one of my brothers was posting videos to YouTube and my husband was helping behind the scenes. I started getting more and more subscribers, and in our state of shock, my husband convinced me to continue making videos with his help.

Being a bit scared and unsure of how to begin, I started creating fashion videos, then shifted to some family recipe videos—Mexican rice being the first. The feedback was amazing. People were watching and loving it, even though the camera was shaky and the video wasn't the best quality. This is when we realized cooking is what I should be focusing on. So I started sharing more and more family recipes on YouTube, and after a few short months, I was able to create content full time.

My husband and I have been a team since day one. He simply doesn't get the credit he deserves. He honestly has the harder job in making sure the lighting, audio, and camera angles are all perfect as well as capturing and editing the best photos of the food. He does it all! Our perfect teamwork is what has allowed us to do this for all these years.

I've always had a passion for cooking. My favorite way to show love to my family is through food. Seeing the happiness that comes from a full belly always fills my heart with so much joy. Looking back, when I started cooking real dishes at age twelve, I almost burned down

the house. It's funny now, but at the time, oh, I was scared. But like we say: *Echando a perder se aprende* (you learn it by spoiling it). I learned how to cook with lots and lots of practice—just like anything else in life.

I've been able to learn a lot from my mom, my grandma, and my husband through his mom's recipes. I particularly loved spending time with my grandma in the kitchen. We'd talk and she'd pass down to me all her tips and tricks. If you come from a Mexican household, you know grandmas and moms don't give exact measurements. They go with *con un poquito de esto y un puntito del otro* (a little bit of this and a pinch of that). That's how I learned, and yes, the recipes were delicious, but sometimes it would taste better one day and needed more of something another day. This is how I realized my recipes needed to include exact measurements as often as possible, so when people make them they taste just as delicious every single time. I wanted to show how easy and fun cooking can be, that cooking doesn't have to be complicated, and that we can all make our moms (or whoever taught us) proud! When people think of Mexican food, they think of hours in the kitchen—and that's simply not the case.

All these years later, I see comments on my videos from people who try my recipes and love how they turn out. Some even convert the picky eaters in their families with my recipes. Seeing comments like these fills my heart with so much joy and fuels me to continue doing what I'm doing.

I always knew I wanted to help others. Sure, I no longer help others by making them feel pretty or assisting them with their health care, but now I'm helping people bring their families together with recipes anyone can enjoy. I'm so proud and honored to be sharing my authentic Mexican recipes that continue to be favorites not only in my household, but also in many others.

Each recipe is special and I hope you find something to love about every single one of them. If there is one thing I want you to take away from this book and these recipes, it's to never forget to include one extra serving of love!

The Regalado-Mendoza Family

"Most of my recipes have been passed down from generation to generation and have become favorites in not only my family but also many others—and I hope they become yours too!"

"I've always had a passion for cooking. My favorite way to show love to my family is through food. Seeing the happiness that comes from a full belly always fills my heart with so much joy!"

My
Kitchen
Essentials

Equipment..24

Ingredients...26

Roasting Steps & Techniques...............31

Equipment

The recipes in this book sometimes call for equipment that might be unfamiliar to someone new to Mexican cuisine. Before we start cooking, let's dive into some information on the types of equipment you can expect to find.

Comal

A comal is a flat griddle used to cook tortillas, sopes, and gorditas, as well as to roast peppers and spices.

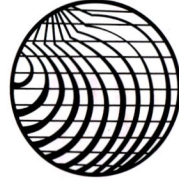

Concha Cutter

A concha cutter is a stamp tool in the shape of a shell that is used to give conchas their shape.

Molcajete

A molcajete is a mortar and pestle made from volcanic rock that is used to grind or pulverize spices and to make salsas. This tool can also be used as a serving dish.

Molinillo

A molinillo is a wooden whisk used to mix and froth Mexican hot chocolate or champurrado.

Tortilla Press

Made from cast iron, aluminum, or wood, a tortilla press is used to flatten masa to make tortillas or sopes. It is also perfect for pressing down the toppings on conchas.

Tortilla Warmer

A tortilla warmer is a basket or container full of tortillas served at the table to keep them fresh, soft, and warm.

Ingredients

Mexican cuisine calls for many ingredients you might not often see in other recipes. The following is more information about these ingredients—all of which are in recipes in this book.

Herbs, Spices & Others

Perfect to always have in your pantry, these ingredients are very common in many Mexican recipes. The flavors in these spices will bring each dish to the next level.

Mexican Oregano

This is an herb that's very popular in many Mexican dishes. It's perfect for broths, menudo, pozoles, sauces, and adobos, especially birria. Before using, make sure you activate it by rubbing it in your hands until fragrant.

Ground Cumin

I love using this spice in many of my dishes—from rice to enchiladas to meats to adobos. This flavorful spice can quickly overpower your dish, so be very careful and precise when using it.

Bay Leaves

These are very aromatic and smell similar to oregano. Very common in many dishes, they can be used fresh or dried.

Whole Cloves

Whole cloves are flower buds from an evergreen tree. Perfect for meat rubs, marinades, and syrups, a few cloves can go a long way.

Piloncillo

Unrefined whole cane sugar, piloncillos are aromatic, unique in flavor, and often used to make simple syrups and drinks.

Mexican Chocolate

Made with cacao, sugar, and cinnamon, Mexican chocolate is uniquely flavorful and perfect for many drinks and mole dishes. Two commonly found brands are Abuelita and Ibarra. Mexican chocolate is usually sold in round tablets or as a finely ground powder.

Quesos & Creams

Quesos and creams are very crucial to most of my dishes. Each cheese has a purpose and helps to bring the dish together in a flavorful way, and the cream is, in most cases, the cherry on top.

Queso Oaxaca

Often found wrapped in a ball, queso oaxaca is a great melting cheese. It might look like mozzarella, but the melt is much better.

Queso Fresco

Fresh, salty, crumbly, and creamy, queso fresco is similar in texture and flavor to ricotta. This cheese is perfect for tacos or enchiladas.

Queso Cotija

This cheese is similar to Parmesan but creamier. The salty flavor and crumbly texture allows it to pair well with corn on the cob, sopes, tacos, refried beans, and more.

Queso Panela

With a mild flavor and creamy texture, this is the best cheese to use for grilling or crumbling over soups, such as Sopa de Fideo con Carne (page 130).

Crema Mexicana

This everyday table cream complements enchiladas, tacos, gorditas—basically every Mexican dish! This cream also works as a base for desserts, such as Gelatina Fresas con Crema (page 224).

Ingredients

Peppers & Tomatillos

Peppers are a staple in nearly every recipe I make. There are various types and each one has its own unique purpose. (When using dried pepper pods, make sure to rinse them well, remove the seeds and stem, and, if necessary, roast in vegetable oil.)

Poblano Peppers

Also known as ancho peppers when dried, poblano peppers are perfect in sauces and adobos, and they assist in intensifying the colors of a dish when dried. They must be roasted if used fresh.

Guajillo Peppers

These are some of the most common peppers used when making any red sauce or adobo. They're fruitier in taste, with zero spice. They work well as New Mexico pepper substitutes when a milder spice level is preferred. Hydrate them well and avoid overcooking them or a bitter flavor will form.

New Mexico Peppers

New Mexico peppers are hands down my favorite peppers to use when making menudo, pozole, birria, mole, or literally any dish that requires red dried peppers. They're spicy and can be toasted to bring an extra layer of flavor to any sauce, but be very careful not to overcook as it will allow a bitter flavor to come through.

Arbol Peppers

Arbol peppers are even spicier than New Mexico peppers and they're the only peppers I don't remove the seeds from. A few peppers will go a long way! Roast them for some extra flavor, but be careful not to burn them.

Chipotle Peppers

Chipotle peppers are basically jalapeños that have been dried and smoked. Not only do these peppers add spicy notes to a dish, but they also provide a nice smoky flavor. Found dried or in adobo sauce, these peppers are best used in recipes like my Barbacoa de Res (page 150) and Camarónes a la Diabla (page 198).

Serrano Peppers

Serrano peppers are my favorite fresh peppers to use when making salsas or sauces. This is another spicy pepper, so a few of these go a long way in any dish.

Anaheim Peppers

These are great to use to make sauces and salsas. They need to be roasted before use and they can work great as a substitute for the poblano peppers in my Chile Rellenos (page 206) recipe.

Tomatillos

Tomatillos (Mexican husk tomatoes) are small green tomatoes with peels that need to be removed before cooking. After you peel them, wash the tomatillos until the skin is no longer sticky. Overcooking them will cause a bitter taste, so be sure to cook them only until they become yellowish in color. When boiling, don't allow them to burst.

Roasting Steps & Techniques

Many recipes in this book require roasted peppers, tomatoes, or spices. Roasting is essential for many of these ingredients to become as flavorful and as complementary to the other ingredients in the recipes as possible. Here's how to do it.

Green Peppers

When roasting green peppers (poblano, Anaheim, serrano, jalapeño), the goal is to enhance the flavor and help remove the outer layer to assist in the cleaning, deseeding, and deveining process.

Start by following one of these methods:

- **Gas stove:** Place the peppers on a wire rack and roast them over an open flame until charred on both sides.
- **Electric stove:** Place the peppers on a comal and roast over medium heat until charred on both sides.
- **Broiler:** Place the peppers on a lightly oiled baking sheet and roast on medium heat until blackened on both sides.

Place the roasted peppers in a resealable plastic bag and allow to sweat for at least 15 minutes. After 15 minutes, remove the peppers from the bag, then deseed and devein.

Tomatoes & Tomatillos

When roasting tomatoes or tomatillos, follow one of the cooking methods in the "Green Peppers" section. But unlike the peppers, bagging and sweating aren't required. The tomatoes will soften sufficiently during the roasting process.

Dried Peppers & Spices

When roasting dried peppers and spices, follow one of the cooking methods in the "Green Peppers" section (but without using the wire rack over the open flame) and roast quickly—about 30 seconds or until fragrant—to prevent burning. Bagging and sweating aren't required.

Drinks

Agua Fresca de Pepino con Limon 34

Agua Fresca de Hibisco con Fresas 36

Agua Fresca de Piña Colada 38

Agua Fresca de Sandia y Pepino 40

Café de Olla Helado 42

Café de Olla 44

Horchata de Fresa 45

Horchata 46

Horchata de Chocolate 48

Atole de Galletas 50

Champurrado 52

Ingredients

4 medium cucumbers, peeled and chopped into large chunks

5 cups water, divided

⅓ cup freshly squeezed lime juice

For the simple syrup

¾ cup granulated sugar

¾ cup water

For serving

ice cubes

Agua Fresca de Pepino con Limon

Cucumber & Lime Water

✦ **Makes** 8 cups   ✦ **Ready in** 30 minutes

This has to be the most refreshing drink you can make. It's perfect for quenching thirst on a hot summer day and it's a must-have at backyard family gatherings. There's nothing better to keep you and your guests happy and refreshed! For adult gatherings, consider adding tequila and jalapeños for an extra kick!

1 To make the simple syrup, in a small saucepan over medium heat, combine the sugar and water. Stir until fully dissolved and bring to a simmer. Once simmering, turn off the heat and allow the syrup to cool to room temperature.

2 In a blender, combine the cucumbers and 2½ cups of water. Blend on high until fully combined.

3 Use a fine-mesh strainer to strain the mixture from the blender into a large pitcher. Discard the remaining pulp.

4 Add the lime juice, simple syrup, and the remaining 2½ cups of water. Stir well until fully combined. Serve over ice.

Ingredients

12 cups water, divided
2 cups granulated sugar
2 cups dry hibiscus flowers
15 ripe strawberries, washed
and tops removed
juice of 1 lime

For serving

ice cubes

Agua Fresca de Hibisco con Fresas

Strawberry Hibiscus Water

✦ **Makes** 1 gallon
✦ **Ready in** 10 minutes

Refreshing, fragrant, and beautiful in color, this is a very popular Mexican drink made with hibiscus flowers. The strawberries enhance its vibrant color and overall sweetness. My mom keeps a pitcher of this in her fridge at all times because it's so delicious and complements many of our favorite Mexican dishes.

1   In a medium saucepan over medium heat, bring 6 cups of water to a boil.

2   Add the sugar and mix until dissolved. Remove the pan from the heat and add the hibiscus flowers, allowing them to steep for 20 minutes.

3   Use a fine-mesh strainer to strain the mixture into a large pitcher. Discard the hibiscus flowers.

4   In a blender, combine the strawberries and 4 cups of water. Blend on high until liquefied. Strain the mixture into the pitcher and discard the remaining pulp.

5   Add the lime juice and the remaining 2 cups of water. Stir well to combine. Serve over ice.

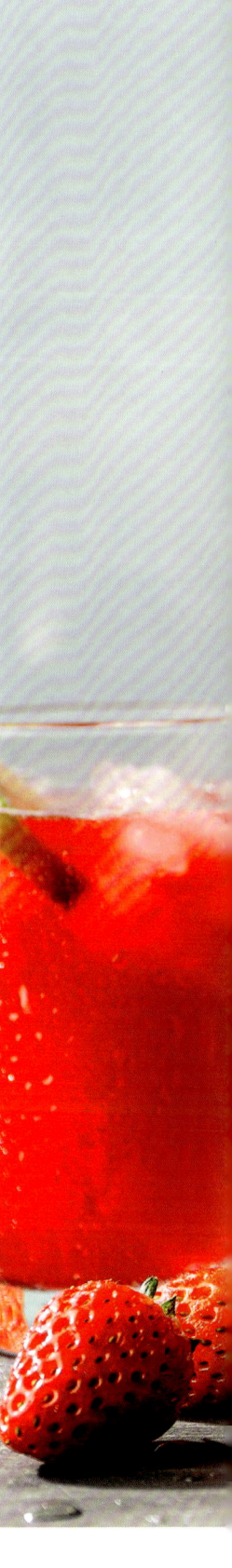

Ingredients

3 pineapples, peeled, cored and chopped (see Note), plus wedges for garnishing (optional)

4½ cups cold water, divided

1 (15oz [425g]) can of cream of coconut

1 (11oz [312g]) can of sweetened condensed coconut milk (see Note)

For serving

ice cubes

maraschino cherries

Agua Fresca de Piña Colada

Creamy Pineapple and Coconut Water

◆ **Makes** 12 cups   ◆ **Ready in** 5 minutes

This creamy drink is delicious and super easy to make for spring and summer gatherings. Consider adding some rum if you're entertaining adults or looking for a little extra kick. It's seriously so tasty and only requires a few ingredients! Who doesn't love a refreshing piña colada on a hot day?

1   In a large blender, combine the pineapple and 2 cups of water. Blend on high until liquefied. You might need to blend in batches.

2   Use a fine-mesh strainer to strain the mixture into a pitcher. Discard the remaining pulp.

3   Add the cream of coconut and coconut milk to the blender. Blend on high until fully mixed.

4   Add the coconut mixture and the remaining 2½ cups of water to the pitcher of pineapple and water blend. Stir well to combine.

5   Garnish with a pineapple wedge and maraschino cherries (if using). Serve with ice.

Note

The pineapple and water from step 1 can be substituted for 2 quarts (1.9L) of pineapple juice if you're looking to save time. Make sure to only use 2½ cups of water in step 4 if you make this substitution.

While I recommend sweetened condensed coconut milk, you might want to use unsweetened milk if you prefer your drinks less sweet.

Ingredients

1 medium or 2 mini seedless watermelon, peeled and chopped, divided
1 medium cucumber, peeled and chopped
juice of 2 lemons
3 cups water

For the simple syrup
¾ cup granulated sugar
¾ cup water

For serving
ice cubes

Agua Fresca de Sandia y Pepino

Watermelon and Cucumber Water

~~~~~~~~~~~~~~~~~~~~~~~~~~~~~~~~

◆ **Makes** 8 cups
◆ **Ready in** 30 minutes

~~~~~~~~~~~~~~~~~~~~~~~~~~~~~~~~

Watermelon and cucumber are my two preferred snacks when I'm craving something refreshing. Now think of that combination in a drink! My favorite beverage to enjoy in the summertime, this delectable blend is the best way to beat the heat. I'd drink this agua fresca year-round if only watermelon were always in season!

1   To make the simple syrup, in a small saucepan over medium heat, combine the sugar and water. Stir until fully dissolved and bring to a simmer. Once simmering, turn off the heat and allow the syrup to cool to room temperature.

2   In a blender, combine the watermelon, cucumber, and lemon juice. Blend on high until smooth.

3   Use a fine-mesh strainer to strain the mixture into a large pitcher. Discard the remaining pulp.

4   Add the simple syrup and water to the pitcher. Stir well until fully combined. Serve with ice.

Café de Olla Helado

Iced Coffee

✦ **Makes** 8 cups
✦ **Ready in** 7 hours

Ingredients

2–3 cups granulated coffee
  (such as Folgers)
¼ cup ground cinnamon
1 cinnamon stick
4 whole star anise
8 whole cloves
8 cups water, divided
1 (8oz [227g]) piloncillo block or
  1 cup light brown sugar

For serving

ice cubes
whole milk, to taste

As a little girl, I used to love waking up to the smell of café de olla (spiced coffee). As soon as I smelled it, I knew I was about to have a good day. My grandma used to give us a cup for breakfast, along with some pan dulce (sweet bread). As an adult, a cup of iced coffee during the summer is a must, but I still want to taste all the spiced flavors café de olla brings together.

1   Use cheesecloth to make a bundle with the coffee, ground cinnamon, cinnamon stick, star anise, and cloves. Tie the homemade tea bag together with twine. Add the bundle and 7 cups of water to a large pitcher or jar. Let steep for 7–10 hours.

2   In a medium saucepan over medium heat, combine the piloncillo and the remaining 1 cup of water. Heat until the piloncillo fully dissolves. Remove the saucepan from the heat.

3   Remove the bundle from the pitcher, squeeze out any excess water, and discard. Add the saucepan mixture and stir well. Serve with ice and add milk to taste.

Ingredients

4 cups water

1 (8oz [227g]) piloncillo block or
   1 cup light brown sugar

1 cinnamon stick

2 whole cloves

2 whole star anise

¼ cup granulated instant
   coffee (such as Nescafé),
   plus more to taste

Café de Olla

Spiced Coffee

✦ **Makes** 5 cups   ✦ **Ready in** 10 minutes

Café de olla is traditionally brewed in a large clay pot, but we're using a saucepan for this recipe. My grandma used to make this for me when I was a little girl. A clay pot always sat on her stovetop, ready to serve. This drink is perfect to enjoy in the morning with conchas (shell-shaped sweet bread) or donas (donuts). I typically serve this to guests and they always ask for more.

1   In a medium saucepan over medium heat, combine the water, piloncillo, cinnamon stick, cloves, and star anise. Bring to a boil, stirring until the piloncillo is completely dissolved. Remove the saucepan from the heat.

2   Stir the instant coffee (adding more to taste) in to the saucepan and mix well. Use a fine-mesh strainer to strain the mixture into a mug. Serve hot.

Horchata de Fresa

Strawberry Horchata

~~~~~~

◆ **Makes** 10 cups   ◆ **Ready in** 4 hours

~~~~~~

If you love strawberries and horchata as much as I do, you're going to love this delicious strawberry horchata. The combination of the sweet, bright-red berries with the rich, creamy classic horchata creates a very delicious and refreshing drink. The best part is you can make it all year long!

1   Wash and rinse the rice. In a medium bowl, combine the rice, hot water, and cinnamon stick. Cover and allow to soak for at least 4 hours, but preferably overnight.

2   In a large blender, combine the soaked rice mixture and sugar. Blend on high until smooth. You might need to blend in batches.

3   Use a fine-mesh strainer to strain the mixture into a medium jar or pitcher. Discard anything left in the strainer. Rinse out the blender and clean the strainer.

4   In the cleaned blender, combine the strawberries and 1 cup of whole milk. Blend on high until smooth.

5   Use the cleaned fine-mesh strainer to strain the strawberry mixture into the pitcher. Discard the seeds.

6   Add the vanilla extract, the cans of milk, and the remaining 3 cups of whole milk. Stir well to combine. Serve over ice.

Ingredients

1½ cups uncooked white rice
4 cups hot water
1 small cinnamon stick
¾ cup granulated sugar
1lb (454g) strawberries, washed and halved
4 cups whole milk, divided
1 tsp pure vanilla extract
1 (14oz [397g]) can of sweetened condensed milk
1 (12oz [340g]) can of evaporated milk

For serving
ice cubes

Ingredients

1½ cups uncooked white rice

4 cups hot water

1 large cinnamon stick

¾ cup granulated sugar

1 tsp pure vanilla extract

1 (14oz [397g]) can of
 sweetened condensed milk

1 (12oz [340g]) can of
 evaporated milk

4 cups whole milk

For serving

ice cubes

Horchata

✦ **Makes** 10 cups   ✦ **Ready in** 4 hours

Horchata is the tastiest Mexican drink you can make at home. This beverage is made using soaked white rice, cinnamon, and milk. Horchata is my absolute favorite drink because it goes perfectly with almost any Mexican recipe. The best part about this is you can always add different ingredients to change the taste, such as chocolate Abuelita, strawberries, matcha, almonds, coconut, coffee—the list goes on.

1   Wash and rinse the rice. In a medium bowl, combine the rice, hot water, and cinnamon stick. Cover and allow to soak for at least 4 hours, but preferably overnight.

2   In a large blender, combine the soaked rice mixture and sugar. Blend on high until smooth. You might need to blend in batches.

3   Use a fine-mesh strainer to strain the mixture into a medium jar or pitcher. Discard anything left in the strainer.

4   Add the vanilla extract, cans of milk, and whole milk. Stir well to combine. Serve over ice.

Ingredients

1½ cups uncooked white rice

4 cups hot water

1 large cinnamon stick

½ cup sliced almonds

¾ cup granulated sugar

1¼ cup granulated Mexican chocolate (Abuelita or Ibarra)

1 tsp pure vanilla extract

1 (14oz [397g]) can of sweetened condensed milk

1 (12oz [340g]) can of evaporated milk

4 cups whole milk

For serving

ice cubes

Horchata de Chocolate

Chocolate Horchata

◆ **Makes** 10 cups

◆ **Ready in** 4 hours

Ultra-rich, creamy, and sweet, chocolate-flavored horchata is the perfect drink to enjoy with all your favorite desserts or as a dessert on its own. This is my version of "chocolate milk." The combination of rice milk with my favorite chocolate, Abuelita, makes the most refreshing drink, especially if you're a chocolate lover.

1   Wash and rinse the rice. In a medium bowl, combine the rice, hot water, cinnamon stick, and sliced almonds. Cover and allow to soak for at least 4 hours, but preferably overnight.

2   In a blender, combine the soaked rice mixture, sugar, and chocolate. Blend on high until smooth. You might need to blend in batches.

3   Use a fine-mesh strainer to strain the mixture into a medium jar or pitcher. Discard anything left in the strainer.

4   Add the vanilla extract, cans of milk, and whole milk. Stir well to combine. Serve over ice.

Ingredients

1 pack (4.9oz [140g]) of Marias cookies or vanilla cookies, plus more for garnishing

5 cups whole milk, divided

1 tsp Mexican vanilla extract

1 (14oz [397g]) can of sweetened condensed milk

1 (12oz) [340g]) can of evaporated milk

1 4-inch (10 cm) cinnamon stick

For serving

ground cinnamon

Atole de Galletas

Creamy Cookie Atole

⁓⁓⁓⁓⁓⁓⁓⁓⁓⁓⁓⁓⁓⁓⁓⁓⁓⁓⁓⁓⁓⁓⁓⁓⁓⁓⁓

✦ **Makes** 6 cups   ✦ **Ready in** 12 minutes

⁓⁓⁓⁓⁓⁓⁓⁓⁓⁓⁓⁓⁓⁓⁓⁓⁓⁓⁓⁓⁓⁓⁓⁓⁓⁓⁓

Atole is a sweet hot beverage traditionally made from corn masa. This drink is an ideal way to welcome your loved ones during special family gatherings, especially during the holidays. Instead of using corn masa, Marias cookies (Mexican vanilla wafers) are used to thicken up the drink. It's so creamy, smooth, rich, and simply delicious!

1   In a blender, combine the cookies, 1 cup of whole milk, and vanilla extract. Blend on high until smooth. Set aside.

2   In a medium saucepan over medium heat, combine the cans of milk, cinnamon stick, and the remaining 4 cups of whole milk. Bring to a simmer, stirring occasionally.

3   Add the cookie mixture to the simmering milk and cook for about 5 minutes or until slightly thickened. Don't allow the mixture to boil. Remove and discard the cinnamon stick.

4   Garnish with crushed cookies and ground cinnamon. Serve hot.

Ingredients

1 cup instant corn masa flour (Maseca)

1 (12oz [340g]) can of evaporated milk

½ gallon whole milk, divided

5 cups water, divided

2 cinnamon sticks

10 whole cloves

pinch of salt

2 (8oz [227g]) piloncillo blocks

2 Mexican chocolate tablets (Abuelita or Ibarra)

1 tbsp Mexican vanilla blend

Champurrado

Chocolate Atole

✦ **Makes** 15 cups   ✦ **Ready in** 15 minutes

Champurrado is a sweet, hot beverage that's traditionally made from corn masa and is perfect to drink with tamales, for breakfast, or as a dessert. It's also a wonderful drink to enjoy with friends and family during the holidays. With corn masa used to thicken it up, champurrado is creamy, smooth, rich, and delicious! Let me tell you, the combination of the three milks, vanilla, cinnamon, and hot chocolate is simply incredible.

1   In a blender, combine the instant corn masa, evaporated milk, 1 cup of whole milk, and 1 cup of water. Blend on high until smooth.

2   In a large pot over medium heat, combine 4 cups of water, cinnamon sticks, whole cloves, and salt. Bring to a boil. Once boiling, add the piloncillo and allow to fully dissolve.

3   Add the chocolate tablets and stir until fully dissolved. Add the vanilla blend and the remaining milk.

4   Remove the cinnamon sticks and whole cloves. Let the milk heat up for about 6 minutes, stopping before it comes to a boil.

5   Reduce the heat to medium and use a molinillo or whisk to slowly add the contents of the blender. Whisk for 8–10 minutes or until the mixture is thick, creamy, and smooth. Serve hot.

Appetizers & Sides

Ensalada de Calabacita 56

Ceviche de Camarón 58

Coctel de Camarón 60

Ensalada de Pollo 62

Frijoles de la Olla 64

Arroz Blanco 65

Arroz Rojo 66

Espagueti Verde 68

Espagueti Rojo 70

Tortitas de Papa y Queso 72

Ingredients

2 tbsp olive oil

1 red bell pepper, stemmed, seeded, and chopped

3 green onions, thinly sliced

1 to 2 serrano or jalapeño peppers, stemmed, seeded, and minced

3 calabacita (Mexican squash) or zucchini, cubed

1 garlic clove, minced

1 tsp garlic salt

½ tsp freshly ground black pepper

½ tsp onion powder

½ tsp dried oregano

¼ tsp dried parsley

¼ tsp dried thyme

2 avocados, peeled and diced

1 Roma tomato, seeded and chopped

6 tbsp minced fresh cilantro

juice of 1 lemon

salt, to taste

For serving

2 cups crumbled queso fresco

Ensalada de Calabacita

Mexican Squash and Avocado Salad

✦ **Makes** 6 servings

✦ **Ready in** 20 minutes

This recipe screams spring! This light and refreshing calabacita salad brings back so many memories from my childhood. Every year, when my mom would prepare for Lent, I'd look forward to enjoying this salad, especially because I knew she would serve it with tortitas de papa (potato fritters)! I also enjoy serving this with tortilla chips or tostadas.

1   In a medium skillet over medium heat, heat the olive oil. Add the bell pepper, green onions, and serrano pepper(s). Sauté for about 2 minutes, then add the calabacita and garlic. Season with garlic salt, black pepper, onion powder, oregano, parsley, and thyme. Stir to combine.

2   Reduce the heat to low and cook for 5 minutes. Let cool completely.

3   Transfer to a large bowl, then add the avocados, tomato, cilantro, and lemon juice. Salt to taste. Cover and refrigerate until ready to serve.

4   Garnish with queso fresco before serving.

Ingredients

2lb (907g) raw shrimp, cleaned, peeled, deveined, and chopped into bite-size pieces

½ medium red onion, chopped, divided

juice of 4 lemons

juice of 4 limes

½ tsp garlic salt

½ tsp freshly ground black pepper

2 medium cucumbers, peeled, seeded, and chopped

3 Roma tomatoes, seeded and chopped

1 jalapeño pepper, seeded and minced

1 habanero pepper, seeded and minced

1 cup chopped fresh cilantro

½ cup Clamato juice (clam juice)

¼ cup ketchup

2 tbsp Maggi jugo seasoning sauce

salt, to taste

For serving

tostadas

diced avocado

hot sauce (Tapatío or Valentina)

Ceviche de Camarón

Shrimp Ceviche

✦ **Makes** 8 servings   ✦ **Ready in** 2 hours

If you love seafood, lime, and spiciness, you're going to love this delicious ceviche. It's made with shrimp that gets "cooked" from the acidity of the lime and lemon juice, then mixed with peppers, cilantro, cucumber, red onion, and tomatoes. All these ingredients combine for a taste of summer! Because the citrus doesn't actually cook the shrimp, you can always substitute for precooked shrimp if you prefer.

1   In a large bowl, combine the shrimp, half the chopped onion, and the lemon and lime juice. Make sure the juice covers the shrimp completely. Season with garlic salt and black pepper. Cover and refrigerate for 1 hour or until the shrimp turns pink.

2   Pour out half the liquid, then add the cucumbers, tomatoes, jalapeño, habanero, cilantro, Clamato juice, ketchup, seasoning sauce, and the remaining half onion. Stir to combine. Taste for salt and adjust to your liking. Refrigerate for 30 minutes before serving.

3   Serve on top of tostadas. Add diced avocado and hot sauce.

Coctel de Camarón

Shrimp Cocktail

~~~~~~

✦ **Makes** 8 servings   ✦ **Ready in** 1 hour
(plus cooling time)

~~~~~~

Coctel de camarón is a must during Lent and summer. It's so refreshing. The broth from the shrimp and the Clamato are a perfect combination! You can always adjust the spiciness by adding more hot sauce. Serve this delicious cocktail with saltine crackers or tostadas. This recipe calls for whole shrimp, but feel free to chop them up if you prefer them that way.

Ingredients

½ red onion, diced

2 cucumbers, seeded and diced

3 Roma tomatoes, seeded and diced

1 bunch of fresh cilantro, finely chopped

1 jalapeño pepper, seeded and diced

1 habanero pepper, seeded and diced (optional)

For the broth

10 cups water

3 celery sticks

1 Roma tomato

½ white onion

3 garlic cloves

2 tsp shrimp bouillon

1 bay leaf

salt, to taste

4lb (1.8kg) whole raw shrimp, cleaned, peeled, and deveined, shells reserved

For the sauce

3 cups cold Clamato juice or V8

1 cup ketchup

½ cup freshly squeezed lime juice (about 4 limes)

5–10 dashes of Tapatío hot sauce

5–10 dashes of Tabasco hot sauce

freshly ground black pepper, to taste

For serving

chopped avocado

saltine crackers

1   To make the broth, in a Dutch oven or large pot over medium-high heat, combine the water, celery, tomato, onion, garlic, shrimp bouillon, bay leaf, and salt. Bring to a boil and maintain for about 10 minutes.

2   Add the shrimp shells and continue boiling for 5 minutes more.

3   Remove the celery, tomato, onion, garlic, bay leaf, and shrimp shells from the pot. Add the shrimp and cook for 3 minutes more.

4   Remove the Dutch oven or pot from the heat. Fill a large bowl with ice water and transfer the shrimp to the bowl. Set aside. Allow the shrimp to cool in the ice bath and the broth to cool off the heat.

5   To make the sauce, in a large bowl combine 3 cups of the shrimp broth, the Clamato juice, ketchup, lime juice, Tapatío hot sauce, Tabasco hot sauce, and black pepper. Mix well. Taste the cocktail sauce and adjust the seasoning to your liking.

6   Add the red onion, cucumbers, tomatoes, cilantro, peppers, and shrimp. Stir to combine. Refrigerate for at least 30 minutes before serving.

7   Serve with chopped avocado and saltine crackers.

Ingredients

2 garlic cloves

1 white onion, halved

1 tbsp salt

1lb (454g) boneless chicken breasts

3 medium russet potatoes, diced

3 carrots, diced

1 cup frozen peas

4 cups shredded iceberg lettuce

2 to 3 pickled jalapeño peppers, diced

1 (14.5oz [411g]) can of sweet corn kernels, drained

1 cup sour cream

1 cup mayo

¼ cup pickled jalapeño juice

1 tsp freshly ground black pepper

½ tsp garlic salt

For serving

saltine crackers

Ensalada de Pollo

Chicken Salad

✦ **Makes** 8 servings   ✦ **Ready in** 1 hour

Ensalada de pollo is my go-to salad for those days when I'm busy or really don't feel like cooking. This salad is cost effective and perfect for feeding a big family. The best part is you can use whatever you have in your fridge or pantry, but I love the flavor combination of mayo, sour cream, and jalapeño juice. This salad is perfect served in a tostada or with some saltine crackers.

1   Fill a medium pot halfway with water. Set over medium-high heat, then add the garlic, half of the onion, and salt to taste. Bring to a boil, then add the chicken. Remove any scum that floats to the surface, reduce the heat to medium, and let cook for 25 minutes.

2   Transfer the chicken to a large bowl and let cool before shredding. Discard the rest.

3   In a separate saucepan over medium-high heat, combine the potatoes and carrots. Cover with water, add salt to taste, and boil for 5 minutes. Add the peas and cook for 6 minutes more or until the potatoes and carrots are cooked through. Drain and allow to cool completely.

4   Dice the remaining half onion and add to a large bowl. Add the cooked vegetables, lettuce, jalapeños, corn, shredded chicken, sour cream, mayo, jalapeño juice, black pepper, and garlic salt. Mix until well combined. Taste for salt and adjust to your liking. Cover and refrigerate for at least 30 minutes.

5   Serve with saltine crackers.

Tip

You can substitute tuna for chicken for a fun variation of this dish!

Ingredients

4 quarts (3.8L) water (or as much as needed)

½ white onion, finely chopped

2 garlic cloves, crushed

2 bay leaves

1 tbsp chicken bouillon

1½ tsp ground cumin

1½ tsp freshly ground black pepper

salt, to taste

1lb (454g) uncooked dried pinto beans, picked, rinsed, and drained

1 handful of fresh cilantro

1 sprig of fresh thyme (optional)

For serving

queso fresco

crushed chile de árbol peppers

chopped white or red onion

chopped fresh cilantro

Mexican oregano

freshly squeezed lime juice

tortillas

Frijoles de la Olla

Beans in a Pot

✦ **Makes** 8 servings   ✦ **Ready in** 2 hours

This is one of the recipes that reminds me most of my grandma. I remember being only four years old and running to the kitchen to see her big olla de barro (clay pot) sitting on the stovetop. Her beans were always so special. She would top them with fresh cilantro, onion, crushed oregano, lime juice, and queso fresco (on a good day—because queso was a luxury). We'd eat them with freshly rolled tortillas de maiz (corn tortillas).

1 In a large pot over medium-high heat, combine the water, onion, garlic, bay leaves, chicken bouillon, cumin, black pepper, and salt. Bring to a boil.

2 Add the beans, cilantro, and thyme. Reduce the heat to medium-low and simmer gently for 2 to 3 hours or until the beans are tender, stirring occasionally. Add more hot water as needed to keep the beans covered.

3 Remove the bay leaves and sprig of thyme and add the bean mixture to individual serving bowls and top with queso fresco, chile de árbol, onion, cilantro, Mexican oregano, freshly squeezed lime juice, and some of the liquid from the beans. Serve with tortillas on the side.

Arroz Blanco

White Rice

✦ **Makes** 6 servings ✦ **Ready in** 30 minutes

White rice is a staple in my kitchen. This rice is so flavorful—it's wonderful to enjoy by itself or as a simple side dish to complement any Mexican main dish, such as **Camarónes a la Diabla** (page 198). Easy, versatile, and tasty, you can't go wrong with white rice!

1   In a large nonstick pan over medium-high heat, combine the oil and butter. Heat until the butter melts.

2   Add the onion, pepper, and garlic. Sauté for 3 minutes, then add the rice and fry for about 2 minutes.

3   Add the water, chicken bouillon, garlic salt, and vegetables. Stir well and bring to a simmer. (Taste and adjust the salt as needed.)

4   Reduce the heat to low, cover, and cook for 15 minutes. (Do not uncover or mix.)

5   Turn off the heat and let sit covered on the burner for 10 minutes before serving.

Ingredients

2 tbsp vegetable oil

1 tbsp unsalted butter

½ small white onion, finely chopped

½ jalapeño or serrano pepper, finely chopped

1 garlic clove, minced

1½ cups uncooked enriched extra-long grain rice

3 cups water or chicken broth

2 tsp chicken bouillon

1½ tsp garlic salt, plus more to taste

1 cup mixed vegetables (frozen or canned)

salt, to taste

Ingredients

3 Roma tomatoes, halved

¼ small white onion

¼ small red bell pepper
(optional)

1 garlic clove

2 tsp chicken bouillon

2 tsp tomato bouillon

½ tsp ground cumin

1 tsp salt, plus more to taste

2 cups water

¼ cup vegetable oil

2 cups uncooked white rice
(Mahatma)

1 cup mixed vegetables (frozen
or canned) (optional)

Arroz Rojo

Red Rice

⁓⁓⁓⁓⁓⁓⁓⁓⁓⁓⁓⁓⁓⁓⁓⁓

✦ **Makes** 8 servings

✦ **Ready in** 30 minutes

⁓⁓⁓⁓⁓⁓⁓⁓⁓⁓⁓⁓⁓⁓⁓⁓

Arroz rojo is a staple in Mexican cuisine. In fact, it's a very commonly served side dish that complements any Mexican main. I'm not going to lie: Learning how to make rice was one of the hardest things for me. I often burned it or undercooked it, but once I mastered it, there was no going back! We love rice with all our main dishes and my kids enjoy it with a couple spoonfuls of sour cream mixed in.

1   In a blender, combine the tomatoes, onion, bell pepper, garlic, chicken bouillon, tomato bouillon, cumin, salt, and water. Blend on high until smooth. (This should make about 4 cups.)

2   In a medium pan over medium-high heat, heat the oil. Add the rice and fry until lightly golden brown, about 5 minutes, stirring frequently.

3   Add the tomato broth, stirring continuously, then add the vegetables (if using). Taste the broth for salt and adjust as needed.

4   Bring to a simmer, then reduce the heat to low. Cover and allow to cook for 25 minutes.

5   Remove the pan from the heat and allow the rice to rest covered for 5 minutes. Fluff with a fork before serving.

For the sauce

3 large poblano peppers, roasted, seeded, and peeled

1 serrano pepper, roasted, seeded, and peeled

¼ white onion, roasted

1 garlic clove

1 handful of fresh cilantro

½ cup shredded Monterey Jack or queso Oaxaca

4oz (113g) cream cheese

2 cups crema Mexicana

¾ cup whole milk

1½ tsp chicken bouillon

1½ tsp freshly ground black pepper

½ tsp garlic salt, plus more to taste

1 tbsp unsalted butter

For the spaghetti

¼ white onion

2 dried bay leaves

salt, to taste

16oz (454g) uncooked spaghetti

For serving

queso fresco

Espagueti Verde

Green Spaghetti

✦ **Makes** 6 servings ✦ **Ready in** 25 minutes

Espagueti verde is a family favorite. You can never go wrong with a plate of green spaghetti topped with queso fresco. Enjoy it by itself or served as a side with your favorite source of protein. This spaghetti is so cheesy, creamy, and flavorful— and you can make it as spicy as you like. Poblano peppers are flavorful but not very spicy, so I like to add a serrano pepper for a little hit of spice, making this a recipe the whole family can enjoy!

1   In a blender, combine the poblano peppers, serrano pepper, roasted onion, garlic, cilantro, shredded cheese, cream cheese, crema Mexicana, milk, chicken bouillon, black pepper, and garlic salt. Blend on high until smooth.

2   Fill a large pot with water and add the onion, bay leaves, and salt. Bring to a boil, add the spaghetti, and cook the pasta according to the package directions. When the pasta is al dente, reserve ½ cup of pasta water and set aside until ready to use. Discard the remaining water, onion, and bay leaves.

3   In a skillet over medium heat, melt the butter. Add the poblano sauce and pasta water, and adjust the salt to your liking. Bring to a simmer and maintain for 5 minutes. Add the spaghetti, reduce the heat to low, and cook for 5 minutes more.

4   Top with queso fresco before serving.

For the spaghetti

¼ white onion

2 dried bay leaves

salt, to taste

16oz (454g) uncooked
    spaghetti

For the sauce

3 Roma tomatoes, halved

¼ small white onion

2 chipotle peppers in adobo
    sauce

1 garlic clove

4oz (113g) cream cheese, room
    temperature

½ cup shredded queso
    Oaxaca

1 tbsp unsalted butter

For serving

queso fresco

Espagueti Rojo

Red Spaghetti

✦ **Makes** 6 servings   ✦ **Ready in** 25 minutes

Espagueti rojo is often served with **Asado de Boda** (page 104), **Mole de Olla** (page 126), or **Chile Verde** (page 120), but it goes great with any Mexican main dish. This spaghetti is a must-have at our gatherings—everyone who tries it always asks for more because it's so irresistible. The tomato broth mixed with the cheese makes it so cheesy and creamy, and my kids love to eat it with queso fresco on top! You can never go wrong with this simple yet delicious red spaghetti.

1   To make the spaghetti, fill a large pot with water and add the onion, bay leaves, and salt. Bring to a boil, add the spaghetti, and cook the pasta according to the package directions. When the spaghetti is al dente, reserve 2½ cups of pasta water and set aside until ready to use. Discard the remaining water, onion, and bay leaves.

2   To make the sauce, in a blender, combine the tomatoes, onion, chipotle peppers and adobo sauce, garlic, cream cheese, queso Oaxaca, and pasta water. Blend on high until smooth.

3   In a skillet over medium heat, melt the butter. Add the blended mixture and bring to a simmer. Adjust the salt to your liking and let simmer for 5 minutes. Add the spaghetti, reduce the heat to low, and cook for 5 minutes more.

4   Top with queso fresco before serving.

Ingredients

7 medium russet potatoes, rinsed, peeled, and halved
salt, to taste
1 tsp freshly ground black pepper
½ tsp dried cilantro
1 tsp garlic powder
1 tsp onion powder
1 tsp dried oregano
½ tsp dried parsley
1 tbsp cornstarch
2 large eggs, beaten
2 cups shredded queso Oaxaca or your favorite melting cheese
1 cup queso cotija
1 handful of fresh cilantro, finely chopped
3 green onions, finely chopped
1 cup vegetable oil

Tortitas de Papa y Queso

Cheesy Potato Cakes

✦ **Makes** 16 tortitas   ✦ **Ready in** 1 hour

These are the perfect appetizer. They're seriously delicious—the cheesy crust makes them crispy on the outside and super soft on the inside. It's a crowd pleaser for sure! Although it's perfect to enjoy during Lent, you can also serve this as a main dish with a side of **Ensalada de Calabacita** (page 56)!

1   In a large pot, add the potatoes, cover with water, and add the salt. Bring to a boil over medium-high heat, then reduce the heat to medium-low and continue cooking for 30–35 minutes or until the potatoes are fork-tender. Drain the water, transfer the potatoes to a large bowl, and let cool. Once cool, smash the potatoes down.

2   Season the potatoes with salt, black pepper, cilantro, garlic powder, onion powder, oregano, parsley, and cornstarch. Mix well, then add the eggs, Oaxaca cheese, cotija cheese, cilantro, and green onions. Stir to combine.

3   To a medium frying pan over medium heat, add enough oil to cover half a tortita, or about ½ inch (1.3 cm). Allow the oil to heat as you form the tortitas.

4   Form the tortitas by using a measuring cup. Scoop up the potato mixture, then use your hands to roll the mixture into a ball. Use the palms of your hands to press the ball into a patty. Repeat with the rest of the potato mixture.

5   Place a few tortitas into the hot oil, making sure not to overcrowd them. Cook until the bottoms are golden brown, about 3 minutes, then carefully flip the tortitas over and cook for 3 minutes more.

6   Line a large plate with a paper towel, then transfer the tortitas to the plate. Remove any remaining tortita mixture from the pan before frying the next batch, then repeat the process of frying the rest of the tortitas. Serve hot.

Tortillas & Bread

Pan Bolillo 76

Concha 78

Masa Basica para Antojitos .... .80

Masa para Tamales 81

Donas Mexicanas 82

Tortillas de Harina 84

Tortillas de Maiz 86

Ingredients

4 cups all-purpose flour, plus more for work surface

2 tsp granulated sugar

2 tsp salt

1 tbsp dry instant yeast

4 tbsp vegetable shortening

1¾ cups warm water (110°F [43°C])

2 tbsp vegetable oil, for greasing

Pan Bolillo

Mexican Rolls

✦ **Makes** 8 bolillos   ✦ **Ready in** 2 hours

This type of Mexican bread roll is shaped like a football. Crusty on the outside but super soft on the inside, bolillo is used in many ways, such as for tortas, buttered and dunked in **Menudo** (page 122), or simply enjoyed alone with coffee or **Champurrado** (page 52). Similar in taste to a baguette, homemade bolillo is made with only a few ingredients—many of which you should already have in your pantry!

1   In a stand mixer fitted with the dough hook attachment, combine the flour, sugar, salt, instant yeast, and vegetable shortening. Begin to mix on medium speed until the shortening has crumbled and combined with the flour. It should look and feel like sand. (See Note.)

2   Decrease to the lowest speed and slowly add in the water.

3   Increase the speed to medium and knead for 10 minutes or until the dough has an elastic consistency. It should feel sticky. Do not add more flour.

4   Transfer the dough to a bowl greased with vegetable oil. Rub a little more oil on top of the dough to prevent it from drying. Cover with plastic wrap and a kitchen towel. Place in a warm spot and allow to rest for 1 hour.

5   Punch the air out of the dough. Add flour to a clean work surface and transfer the dough. Knead the dough for 1 minute.

6   Shape the dough into a flat circle and divide into 8 evenly sized portions. Roll each divided portion of dough into a ball and transfer to a greased baking sheet. Once all 8 have been formed and placed on the sheet, cover with a kitchen towel and allow to rest for 10 minutes.

7   Stretch out a dough ball to form a long oval. Begin by grabbing the end and gently slamming it against the countertop about 10 times, alternating ends. Repeat with the other dough balls.

8   Shape the dough to form the bolillo. Grab the end of the dough oval, fold it inward, and press down. Fold in the dough to the left and right of where you pressed down. Grab the new end you just folded in and repeat the process until the oval has been rolled into a log of dough. Gently roll the dough log back and forth, putting pressure on the ends to push the dough toward the middle, creating a football shape. Don't press down on the center of the log. Dust the log with flour. Repeat with the remaining dough.

Note

If you don't have a stand mixer, you can knead with your hands. Simply knead and trust the process. Don't add any more flour to the dough.

9   Transfer the bolillo to a greased baking sheet and brush a little oil on top of each. Cover with a kitchen towel and allow to rise for 30 minutes.

10 Preheat the oven to 350°F (180°C). Use a sharp knife to cut a ¼-inch-deep (0.65 cm) slit lengthwise on the top of each loaf.

11 Place a small pan with water in the bottom of the oven. Bake the bread for 25–30 minutes or until golden brown. Allow to cool for at least 5 minutes before serving.

Ingredients

¾ cup warm milk (100–110°F [38–43°C])

1 tbsp dry active yeast

1 tbsp plus ½ cup granulated sugar (½ cup sifted)

4 cups all-purpose flour, sifted

2 tsp ground cinnamon (optional)

¼ tsp salt

3 large eggs, room temperature

1 tbsp pure vanilla extract

6 tbsp unsalted butter, room temperature, plus more for greasing

For the topping

1½ cups all-purpose flour, sifted

1½ cups powdered sugar, sifted

1 cup butter-flavored shortening

1 tbsp pure vanilla extract

2 tbsp cocoa powder

Concha

Mexican Sweet Bread

✦ **Makes** 12 conchas   ✦ **Ready in** 3 hours

Concha is a staple in our kitchen. Of all the pan dulce, conchas continue to be our favorite! Growing up, conchas and coffee were often our breakfast. Very nutritious, right? Let me tell you, it was the best when my grandma always made sure our sweet bread was on the table before we woke up. It might be time consuming, but making this delicious bread at home is well worth it!

1   In a small cup, combine the milk, 1 tablespoon of sugar, and instant yeast. Mix well and allow the yeast to activate, about 7 minutes.

2   On a clean work surface, combine the flour, cinnamon (if using), salt, and the ½ cup sifted sugar. Create a pit in the center of the flour mixture. Add the yeast mixture, whole eggs, and vanilla extract to the pit. Begin to incorporate the dry ingredients into the wet ingredients until fully combined.

3   Knead the dough for 5 minutes. Roll out the kneaded dough and begin adding the butter, kneading as you add. Knead the sticky dough for about 15 minutes more or until it's soft and elastic. Don't add more flour.

4   Grease a large bowl with butter and place the dough inside, flipping it to ensure it's fully greased. Cover with plastic wrap and a kitchen towel. Place in a warm spot to rise until it doubles in size, about 2 hours.

5   To make the topping, in a medium bowl, combine the flour, sugar, shortening, and vanilla extract until a paste forms. Knead the paste until it's soft and doesn't crack. Divide the paste in half. Add the cocoa powder to one half and mix again until incorporated. Form both halves into balls, store them in resealable plastic bags, and set aside.

6   Once the dough has risen, place it on a clean work surface and punch out the air. Shape the dough into a log and cut it into even pieces. (Make 12 if you want average-sized conchas.) Shape each piece of dough into a ball by gently resting your hand on top and rotating counterclockwise. If you find it easier, simply shape the dough into a ball in your hands.

7   Transfer the balls to a greased baking sheet. Grease the top of each with butter and cover them with a kitchen towel.

8   Cut each ball of topping paste into 6 equal pieces. Shape each piece into a small disc and flatten it well. Cover each ball of dough with a flattened paste disc, pressing down so it sticks. Be sure the paste covers the dough completely, along with about 1–2 inches (2.5–5 cm) of extra overlap. The extra paste will ensure the dough is covered after rising.

9   Use a concha cutter or knife to mark each concha. If using a knife, cut about 8 lines into the paste layer on top of each concha. Cover with a kitchen towel and allow the conchas to rest until they double in size, about 45 minutes.

10   Preheat the oven to 350°F (180°C) and bake for 18–20 minutes or until golden. Let rest at least 10 minutes before serving.

Ingredients

4 cups instant corn masa (Maseca)
½ cup all-purpose flour
1½ tsp baking powder
1½ tsp salt
3–3½ cups warm water
1 cup plus 1 tbsp vegetable oil, divided

For the filling/topping

meat of choice
cubed potatoes
beans of choice
shredded lettuce
chopped tomatoes
avocado slices
sour cream
queso fresco
salsa

Tip

To make picaditas: As soon as the masa is off the comal, create a rim around the disc and pinch the inside, creating little hills. Add 1 tbsp vegetable oil to the comal and fry for 2 minutes with your salsa of choice.

To make sopes: As soon as the masa is cooked, use a paper towel to pinch the sides around the edge of each disc to form a rim. Top with beans, meat, and all your favorite toppings.

To make quesadillas: After step 6, add fillings of choice to the flattened dough and fold. Fry until golden brown, about 5 minutes.

Masa Basica para Antojitos

Fried Masa

✦ **Makes** 12   ✦ **Ready in** 40 minutes

A good sope, picadita quesadilla, gordita, huarache, or molote begins with the foundation of the masa—a thick, fried dough. The masa has to be soft on the inside yet a little crispy on the outside. This masa is perfect for all your favorite antojitos. In Mexico, there are many different names for these antojitos, but they're all very similar—they're just shaped and dressed differently. So simple yet so delicious, and you can serve it in so many different ways!

1   In a large bowl, combine the corn masa, flour, baking powder, and salt. As you mix, add the water as you go. Be sure not to add all the water at once.

2   Once the masa flour is completely wet and incorporated, knead for 5 minutes or until it feels thicker and not sticky, like the consistency of Play-Doh. Cover with a damp paper towel or cloth and allow to rest for 20 minutes.

3   Preheat a comal (griddle) over medium heat.

4   In a medium frying pan over medium heat, heat 1 cup of vegetable oil.

5   Roll a medium piece of dough (a little smaller than a tennis ball) into a ball. Flatten with your hands, clapping it back and forth. Make sure it is about ¼-inch (0.65 cm) thick. (A tortilla press works well here if you have one.)

6   Place the flattened dough in the comal and cook for 2 minutes on each side. (See the tip for the picadita variation.) Transfer the dough to the frying pan and fry until golden brown, about 5–6 minutes.

7   Immediately after frying, cut a slit into the side of the fried masa to create a gordita pocket. (See the tip for the sope variation.)

8   Stuff the fried masa with your choice of filling and desired toppings. Repeat with the remaining dough.

Masa para Tamales

Tamale Dough

~~~~~~

◆ **Makes** 36–40 tamales ◆ **Ready in** 2½ hours
(plus 8 hours for soaking corn husks)

~~~~~~

Who doesn't love tamales? Preparing tamales can be a lengthy process, but it's the perfect opportunity to spend quality time with others while you do it. I have so many fond memories of preparing tamales with my grandmother and the rest of the family. While my grandmother is no longer with us, I know she'd be happy I've carried on this tradition with my husband and children.

1   Soak the corn husks in cold water for at least 8 hours.

2   To the bowl of a stand mixer fitted with the paddle attachment, add the lard and beat on medium-high speed for 5 minutes or until creamy.

3   Add the baking powder, 1 cup of masa, and 1 cup of broth. Mix on low speed.

4   Continuing to mix on low speed, add 1 cup of masa and 1 cup of broth at a time until you add the remaining 5 cups of masa and 3 cups of broth. Add the water and mix until combined. Taste a piece of masa and add salt to taste as needed.

5   On medium-high speed, mix for 15 minutes or until the masa is well hydrated. After 15 minutes, the masa should be smooth, airy, and fluffy. Test the masa: Place a piece of masa in a cup of room temperature water (the size doesn't matter). If the masa floats, it's ready. If it sinks, add more broth 2 tablespoons at a time and mix for 2 minutes. Test again until it floats.

6   Remove the paddle attachment and scrape all the masa on the sides down to the bottom. Cover the bowl with a kitchen towel and allow to rest for 20 minutes.

7   Spread the masa over each soaked corn husk, stuff with your filling of choice, fold them into tamales, place the tamales in a prepared steamer pot, and steam for 2 hours before serving.

Ingredients

15oz (425g) corn husks
1½ cups lard
5 tsp baking powder
6 cups instant corn masa (Maseca), divided
4 cups warm broth (about 110°F [43°C]) from cooked meat (see Note), divided, plus more
3 cups warm water (110°F [43°C])
salt, to taste

For the filling
Tamales Verdes (page 189)
Tamales Rojos (page 190)

Note

When making tamales, broth from cooked meat is typically used for an authentic flavor. Store-bought broth will also work for this recipe.

Ingredients

4 cups sifted all-purpose flour, plus more for work surface

½ cup sifted granulated sugar

2 tsp ground cinnamon (optional)

¼ tsp salt

3 large eggs plus 1 egg yolk, room temperature

1 tbsp pure vanilla extract

6 tbsp unsalted butter, room temperature, plus more for greasing

1½ qt vegetable oil, for frying

For the yeast mixture

¾ cup warm milk (100–110°F [38–43°C])

1 tbsp all-purpose flour

1 tbsp granulated sugar

2½ tsp dry active yeast

For the cinnamon sugar

1 cup granulated sugar

2 tbsp ground cinnamon

Donas Mexicanas

Cinnamon Sugar Donuts

✦ **Makes** 18 donuts   ✦ **Ready in** 3½ hours

Mexican donuts are seriously the best when they're homemade—and they're super easy to make! My mom would make a big batch of these delicious donuts for all us kids growing up, and let me tell you, we were the happiest kids on the block. Forget Dunkin' Donuts and Krispy Kreme—these donuts are still my favorite. The best part is that if you want to stuff them with jelly, hazelnut spread, or dulce de leche, you can do so by not making the hole in the center.

1   In a small cup, combine all the yeast ingredients and mix well. Allow to activate, about 7 minutes.

2   On a clean work surface, combine the flour, sugar, cinnamon (if using), and salt. Create a pit in the center of the flour mixture. Add the yeast mixture, eggs, and vanilla to the pit. Begin to incorporate the dry ingredients into the wet ingredients until fully combined.

3   Knead for 10 minutes. Roll out the dough and slowly incorporate the butter, kneading as you go. The dough will be sticky. Knead for 15 more minutes or until the dough is soft and elastic.

4   Grease a large bowl with butter and place the dough inside. Flip the dough to ensure it's fully greased. Cover with plastic wrap and a kitchen towel. Place in a warm area and allow to rise and double in size, about 2 hours.

5   Punch the air out of the dough and transfer to a clean work surface. Shape the dough into a log and divide into two equal halves.

6   Dust the work surface with a little flour and roll one half of the dough out to ½ inch (1.3 cm) thick. Make sure the other half is covered to prevent it from drying out. Roll out the second half after finishing the first one.

7   Use a 2½-inch (6.4 cm) donut cutter, cookie cutter, or a medium cup, begin to cut out the donuts and place them on a greased baking sheet. Cut out the holes using a ¾-inch (1.9 cm) donut cutter. Repeat until donuts have been cut out from both halves. Cover with plastic wrap and allow to rise and double in size, about 45 minutes.

8   In a small bowl, make the cinnamon sugar by mixing together the sugar and cinnamon.

9   In a medium frying pan over medium heat, heat the vegetable oil. Fry 2 donuts at a time until golden brown, about 30 seconds on each side. Remove them from the pan, drain the excess oil, and coat with the cinnamon sugar. Repeat until all the donuts have been fried and coated. Serve warm.

Ingredients

4 cups all-purpose flour, plus more for work surface

2 tsp salt

1½ tsp baking powder

6 tbsp lard, shortening, or butter, plus more

1¼–1½ cups warm water (115°F [46°C])

Tortillas de Harina

Flour Tortillas

✦ **Makes** 12–14 tortillas   ✦ **Ready in** 40 minutes

Nothing tastes better than fresh homemade flour tortillas! I remember when I would come home from school after a bad day, walk into the kitchen, and see a big stack of tortillas my mom made wrapped in the servilleta (napkins), I knew I was going to eat something so delicious. To be honest, when it was time for me to make my own, I struggled. It was very tricky for the perfectionist in me. My mom assured me that practice makes perfect—and she was right!

1   In a large bowl, combine the flour, salt, and baking powder. Add the lard and begin to crumble it with the flour until the mixture looks and feels like sand.

2   Slowly add the water and mix with the flour until the dough comes together and is not dry. Once the dough has formed, knead it on a clean work surface for 5 minutes or until the dough no longer sticks to your hands. The dough should be soft and stretchy.

3   Divide the dough into 12–14 small balls. Rub your hands with lard and lightly pat each ball of dough. This will prevent the dough from drying out. Place the balls of dough on a kitchen towel, cover, and allow to rest for 20 minutes.

4   Preheat a skillet over medium heat.

5   Dust a flat work surface and rolling pin with flour. Dust each ball of dough with flour. Press a ball down with four fingers and use the rolling pin to roll it out, rotating clockwise as you go until it's flat. Flip and roll again, repeating the process until the dough can no longer spread out any farther. At this point, still using the rolling pin, begin rolling from one edge of the dough to the center and back, applying pressure, until the dough is nearly transparent. Rotate and repeat on all sides. It should be about 6 inches (15 cm) wide. Repeat until all the balls of dough have been flattened and formed into uncooked tortillas.

6   Place a tortilla on the skillet and allow to blister, about 15 seconds. Flip and allow to puff, about 30 seconds. Transfer the tortilla to a kitchen towel or a tortilla warmer. Repeat until all the tortillas have been cooked. (It's important to prepare them one at a time to ensure they stay soft and don't dry out.)

7   Serve immediately or store in an airtight container for up to 2–3 days, refrigerated for up to 1 week.

Tortillas de Maiz

Corn Tortillas

Ingredients

- 2 cups instant corn masa flour (Maseca)
- ¼ tsp salt
- 1½–1¾ cups hot water (as hot as your hands can handle)

✦ **Makes** 10 tortillas   ✦ **Ready in** 40 minutes

Corn tortillas are the easiest yet trickiest to master. They're super easy because all you do is mix three ingredients. Yes, only three ingredients! The trickiness comes from needing to ensure they're moist enough, thin enough, and kneaded to perfection. I can't think of any Mexican dish that doesn't taste good with corn tortillas—and let me tell you, homemade is how you do it!

1   In a large bowl, combine the corn masa flour and salt. Slowly begin to pour the water in, mixing while adding to incorporate the flour masa. Don't pour all the water in at once.

2   Once the masa flour is completely wet and incorporated, knead for 5 minutes or until it's firmer and not sticky, like the consistency of Play-Doh.

3   Cover with a damp paper towel or kitchen towel and allow to rest for 20 minutes.

4   Preheat a comal (griddle) over medium heat.

5   Grab a small piece of dough (about 2 tablespoons [35g]) and roll it into a ball. Flatten the ball between two sheets of parchment paper using a flat plate, a grill press on a flat work surface, or a tortilla press. Make sure the uncooked tortilla is as flat and even as possible. (See Note.)

6   Place a tortilla in the hot comal. Cook for 30 seconds, flip, cook another 30 seconds, and flip again. Press down on the center of the tortilla and allow it to puff up.

7   Transfer the tortilla to a kitchen towel or tortillero (tortilla basket) to rest for 5 minutes before serving. Repeat with the remaining dough.

Note

If your tortilla press is uneven, press down one time, flip the tortilla over, and press down again.

Dips & Salsas

Guacamole..90

Pico de Gallo..92

Salsa Macha..94

Salsa Roja..96

Salsa Verde...98

Salsa de Aguacate 100

Chile con Queso Dip..101

Ingredients

2 large ripe avocados

1 Roma tomato, chopped

½ small red onion, diced

1 jalapeño pepper, seeded and diced

½ bunch of fresh cilantro, finely chopped

juice of ½ lime

1 tsp freshly ground black pepper or to taste

1 tsp garlic salt or to taste

Guacamole

- ✦ **Makes** 4 servings
- ✦ **Ready in** less than 5 minutes

This avocado-based dip and spread is an ideal topping for any taco, burrito, quesadilla, torta, or chimichanga. Many also enjoy it with tortilla chips or on a tostada. The best guacamole is homemade, using ingredients you already have in your fridge. I like to serve it as an appetizer or pair it with many of the entrées in this book for a tasty combination of flavors.

1   Slice the avocados in half, remove and discard the pits, and spoon the insides into a large bowl. Dice or smash the avocado in the bowl. Discard the peels.

2   Add the tomato, onion, jalapeño, cilantro, and lime juice. Add the black pepper and garlic salt or season to taste. Mix well to combine.

3   Store in an airtight container in the fridge for up to 3 days or use immediately.

Pico de Gallo

Ingredients

½ white onion, diced

3 Roma tomatoes, diced

½ cup finely chopped fresh cilantro

1 serrano pepper or jalapeño pepper, chopped

juice of 1 large lime

salt, to taste

freshly ground black pepper, to taste

✦ **Makes** 4 servings

✦ **Ready in** 5 minutes

Also known as salsa fresca, pico de gallo is a refreshing salsa made with chopped veggies and seasonings. Sporting the colors of the Mexican flag, pico de gallo complements many favorite Mexican dishes. Regardless of how you enjoy this delicious salsa, you can't deny how flavorful it is!

1   In a large bowl, combine the onion, tomatoes, cilantro, serrano, and lime juice. Season to taste with salt and black pepper.

2   Mix well until combined and refrigerate in an airtight container for 15–20 minutes before serving.

3   Store in an airtight container in the fridge for up to 3 days or use immediately.

Ingredients

1 cup vegetable oil
⅛ white onion
3 garlic cloves
½ corn tortilla
2 tsp sesame seeds
small piece of ancho pepper
25 chile de árbol peppers
½ cup peanuts (optional)
1 tsp salt

Salsa Macha

Spicy Chile Oil Salsa

◆ **Makes** 1 cup　　◆ **Ready in** 20 minutes

Salsa Macha is a spicy salsa that complements pozole, tacos, tostadas, burritos, fried eggs—practically everything! But be warned: This salsa is spicy! I created this recipe using nuts and experimenting with various ingredients, and it turned out great, in my humble opinion. Keep in mind that if you use peanuts, they will replace the tortilla.

1　In a medium frying pan on medium-high heat, add the oil, onion, and garlic, and allow to cook for about 4 minutes.

2　Add the corn tortilla and allow to fry for a few minutes until golden brown and crunchy. (If using peanuts, skip this step.)

3　Remove the tortilla from the pan and turn off the heat. Add the sesame seeds to the pan and allow them to cook until golden brown.

4　Add a small piece of ancho pepper, the chile de árbol peppers, and the peanuts (if using) to the oil and allow to cool down to room temperature.

5　Once cooled, place the contents of the pan and the tortilla and salt into a blender and blend until smooth. Enjoy!

Note

For a less spicy version of this salsa, consider using about 10 chile de árbol peppers.

Salsa Roja

Red Salsa

◆ **Makes** ~1 cup
◆ **Ready in** 15 minutes

A taco needs to have a delicious salsa—that's the rule! This salsa is perfect for all the fried taquitos, street tacos, tortilla chips, or chicharrones one might enjoy. When I was a child, my grandma would make this to sell with chicharrones preparados, a Mexican street food, on the weekends. The fried onion and cilantro enhance the flavor and bring everything together in the best way.

1   To a blender, add the water, tomatoes, chile de árbol peppers, garlic, and salt, and blend until smooth.

2   To a medium frying pan on medium heat, add the oil, onion, and cilantro, and fry until the onion is translucent (about 2 minutes).

3   Add the Mexican oregano and all the contents from the blender to the pan, reduce heat to low, and allow to simmer for 5 minutes until it cooks down. Let cool before serving.

Ingredients

½ cup water
3 Roma tomatoes, roasted
20 chile de árbol peppers
1 garlic clove
2 tsp salt
1 tbsp olive oil
½ small white onion, finely chopped
½ bunch of cilantro, finely chopped
¼ tsp Mexican oregano

Note

You can also make this salsa even easier by boiling the tomatoes (instead of roasting) and chiles, and then blending with water, garlic clove, and salt. Just like that, you have a very delicious salsa roja taquera.

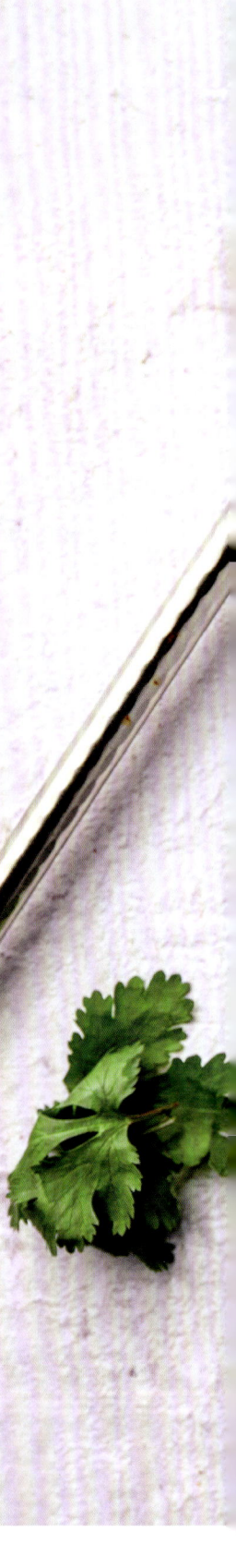

Salsa Verde

Green Salsa

Ingredients

5 tomatillos, peeled and cleaned
5 chile de árbol peppers
1 habanero pepper
1 garlic clove
¼ white onion
¼ cup chopped cilantro
1 tsp salt

✦ **Makes** 1 cup
✦ **Ready in** 10 minutes

This classic salsa is very versatile. Paired with anything from enchiladas to birria, it truly satisfies. In my opinion, this salsa works best with tacos, burritos, tostadas, and tortilla chips. Made with chile de árbol and habanero peppers, this spicy salsa is the only one you'll ever want or need for your tacos!

1   In a medium saucepan over high heat, combine the tomatillos, chile de árbol peppers, habanero pepper, and enough water to submerge everything. Bring to a boil. Once boiling, remove the pan from the heat to cool.

2   Transfer the mixture to a blender. Add the garlic, onion, cilantro, and salt. Blend on high until smooth.

3   Store in an airtight container in the fridge for up to 5 days or serve immediately.

Note

If you prefer a milder salsa, substitute a jalapeño pepper for the habanero pepper and only use 2 chile de árbol peppers.

Ingredients

3 large ripe avocados

3 jalapeño peppers or serrano peppers

3 garlic cloves

¼ small white onion

½ bunch of fresh cilantro

juice of ½ lime

½ tbsp salt

¾–1 cup water or whole milk

Salsa de Aguacate

Avocado Salsa

✦ **Makes** 2 cups   ✦ **Ready in** less than 5 minutes

Avocado salsa is hands down my favorite salsa. It's so creamy and full of flavor! Paired perfectly with taquitos, tacos, chimichangas, nachos, tostadas, or tortilla chips, you can't go wrong with this easy-to-make salsa.

1   Slice the avocados in half, remove and discard the pits, and spoon out the insides. Discard the peels.

2   In a blender, combine the avocados, jalapeños, garlic, onion, cilantro, lime juice, salt, and water. Blend on high until fully combined.

3   Store in an airtight container in the fridge for up to 3 days or use immediately.

Chile con Queso Dip

Chili con Queso Dip

~~~~~~

✦ **Makes** 3 cups   ✦ **Ready in** 10 minutes

~~~~~~

You can serve this as an appetizer, drizzle it on top of chimichangas, taquitos, and enchiladas, or use it as a dip for quesadillas. Regardless of how you choose to serve this queso, believe me when I tell you it's the best! And it's perfect for football season or any gathering with cherished friends and family.

1   In a medium skillet over medium-low heat, melt the butter. Add the flour and paprika and stir together with the butter to make a roux. Add the bell pepper, onion, Anaheim pepper, and jalapeño. Sauté for 3 minutes.

2   Whisk in the enchilada sauce and milk until the mixture begins to thicken up, about 5 minutes. Season with salt to taste.

3   Add in cheese and mix until it completely melts, about 2 minutes. Bring to a simmer, then reduce the heat to low until ready to serve.

Ingredients

3 tbsp salted butter
3 tbsp all-purpose flour
½ tsp smoked paprika
½ red bell pepper, finely chopped
¼ white onion, finely chopped
1 Anaheim pepper, roasted, seeded, and chopped
1 jalapeño pepper, finely chopped
1 (15oz [425g]) can of green enchilada sauce
1½ cup whole milk
salt, to taste
8oz (227g) shredded medium cheddar cheese

Soups & Stews

Asado de Boda.......................104

Birria de Res 106

Caldo de Albóndigas 108

Caldo de Camarón 110

Caldo de Pollo con Arroz..........112

Caldo de Res 114

Carne con Chiles y Papas..........116

Sopa de Conchitas con Pollo 117

Chile Colorado 118

Chile Verde 120

Menudo 122

Pozole Verde de Pollo 124

Mole de Olla 126

Pozole Rojo 128

Sopa de Fideo con Carne..........130

Sopa Azteca 132

Ingredients

5lb (2.3kg) boneless pork shoulder or butt roast, cut into bite-size pieces

2lb (907g) pork ribs

6 tsp salt, plus more to taste

1 tbsp freshly ground black pepper

For the adobo sauce

10½ cups water

1 (3oz [90g]) Mexican chocolate tablet (Abuelita or Ibarra)

4 tbsp vegetable oil

25 New Mexico peppers, cleaned, deseeded, and deveined

3 pasilla peppers, cleaned, deseeded, and deveined

3 garlic cloves

1 **Pan Bolillo roll** (page 76), halved

1 orange, halved

8oz (227g) beer of choice

2 bay leaves

1 tsp dried oregano

1 tsp dried marjoram

1 tsp dried thyme

1 tsp ground cumin

For serving

Mexican rice

Espagueti Rojo (page 70)

Asado de Boda

Red Pork Chili

✦ **Makes** 10 servings   ✦ **Ready in** 2 hours

I'll treasure this dish forever. It was one of the last recipes my grandma taught me while she was still with us. Served at nearly every special occasion, this meal is very popular in our pueblito, Tlahualilo Durango. When I'm invited to a celebration, I know just what will be served: asado de boda with a side of rice and red spaghetti. Waking up to see another day is special enough to celebrate, so I hope you give this recipe a try and enjoy it just as much as we do!

1   In a large Dutch oven over medium-high heat, combine the pork, salt, and black pepper. Cook until the pork has expelled all its juices. Reduce the heat to medium, cover, and cook for 30 minutes more. After 30 minutes, uncover and let sit until the juices evaporate, about 7 minutes.

2   Fry pork in its rendered fat in the Dutch oven until golden brown, about 8–10 minutes.

3   To make the adobo sauce, in a medium pot, bring the water to a boil. Once boiling, add the chocolate tablet and set aside.

4   In a medium frying pan over medium heat, heat the vegetable oil. Once hot, fry each New Mexico pepper and pasilla pepper for 30 seconds on each side before adding to the medium pot.

5   In the same medium pan, fry the garlic cloves, then transfer them to the medium pot. Fry the bolillo in the same medium pan on both sides, then transfer to the medium pot.

6   Transfer all the ingredients from the medium pot to a blender and blend on high until smooth.

7   Add the adobo sauce to the Dutch oven, straining as needed. (You might need to add some water to the blender to thin the sauce enough to pour it out completely.)

8   Squeeze the orange into the Dutch oven. Stir in the squeezed orange, beer, bay leaves, and spices. Add additional salt to taste as needed. Cover and cook for 35–40 minutes or until the pork is fully tender. Remove the orange and bay leaves.

9   Serve with your sides of choice. I recommend rice and **Espagueti Rojo** (page 70) Enjoy!

Ingredients

4½ quarts (4.3L) water
1 white onion, halved
1 head of garlic, halved
2 Roma tomatoes, halved
8 bay leaves, divided
3½ tbsp salt
5lb (2.3kg) chuck pot roast
2lb (907g) beef short ribs

For the adobo sauce

22 New Mexico peppers or guajillo peppers, cleaned and deveined
2 pasilla peppers, cleaned and deveined
5 chile de árbol peppers, stems removed
7 garlic cloves
2 tsp sesame seeds
1½ tsp whole peppercorns
2 tsp Mexican oregano
2 tsp whole cumin
2 tsp dried thyme
5 whole cloves
1-inch (2.5 cm) piece of cinnamon, broken into smaller pieces
1-inch (2.5 cm) ginger root, peeled
4 tbsp distilled white vinegar

For serving

27–30 tortillas
shredded queso Oaxaca cheese
freshly squeezed lime juice
chopped white onion
chopped fresh cilantro

Note

Traditionally, birria has been served alongside rice and beans, but steps 8 and 9 detail how I like to prepare these tacos. Get creative with your own as you see fit!

Birria de Res

Beef Birria

✦ **Makes** 10–12 servings   ✦ **Ready in** 3 hours

Birria is a meat stew that originated in Jalisco, Mexico. While it was traditionally prepared with goat meat, I prefer to prepare it with beef. The broth from this popular recipe is seriously super delicious! You can enjoy this birria as a stew, served with rice, or served in burritos, tortas, or quesadillas or with ramen. My favorite use is as quesabirria tacos, with a side of the flavorful consommé.

1   In a large pot over high heat, combine the water, onion, head of garlic, tomatoes, 4 bay leaves, and salt. Bring to a boil, then add the beef and cook for 20 minutes. Use a strainer to remove any foam or scum that rises to the top of the broth. Reduce the heat to medium-low and cover. Allow to cook for 1 hour.

2   To make the adobo sauce, add the New Mexico peppers, pasilla peppers, and chile de árbol peppers to the large pot. Cook until they soften, about 5–7 minutes. Remove and set aside. Remove and reserve 3 cups of broth.

3   In a small frying pan or skillet over medium-low heat, toast the garlic cloves until fragrant and then set aside with the peppers. Reduce the heat to low and toast the sesame seeds. Once golden, transfer to a blender.

4   To the same frying pan, combine the whole peppercorns, Mexican oregano, cumin, thyme, whole cloves, 4 bay leaves, and cinnamon pieces. Toast until fragrant, about 20 seconds, and then transfer to the blender.

5   Crush the spices down in the bottom of the blender. Add the three kinds of peppers, garlic cloves, reserved broth, ginger root, and white vinegar. Blend on high until smooth.

6   Remove the garlic and onion from the pot. Add the adobo sauce, straining as needed. Stir and taste. Add more salt as needed. Cover and cook for 1½ hours or until the beef is tender.

7   Remove and shred or chop the beef. Use a strainer to remove the top layer from the consommé to remove the grease. If making tacos, reserve some of the grease from the consommé. Return the shredded or chopped beef to the consommé. Either serve alongside Mexican rice and beans, or move to the next steps and prepare tacos.

8   Heat a grill or grill pan to medium heat. Once hot, dip a tortilla into the reserved grease from the consommé. Place the tortilla on the grill, flipping once it blisters. Add the shredded queso Oaxaca. Allow the cheese to melt and the tortilla to crisp. Add beef with a little consommé, freshly squeezed lime juice, onion, and cilantro.

9   Fold in half and serve with a side of consommé and more freshly squeezed lime juice, chopped onion, and cilantro. Repeat for each taco.

Caldo de Albóndigas

Meatball Soup

◆ **Makes** 6 servings   ◆ **Ready in** 45 minutes

This brings up so many beautiful memories of my childhood. My mom would make my siblings and me this soup when she had ground beef to use. It's perfect to enjoy on a cold, rainy day (or any day really). Even the pickiest eater will enjoy this nutritious soup loaded with vegetables. Feel free to mix and match any vegetables you like—and skip the peppers if you prefer your soup less spicy.

Ingredients

For the meatballs

2lb (907g) lean ground beef
1 cup uncooked white rice
2 large eggs, room temperature
¼ white onion, diced
½ cup chopped fresh cilantro or mint
2 garlic cloves, minced
1 chipotle pepper in adobo sauce, minced
2 tsp garlic salt
2 tsp dried oregano
½ tsp salt, plus more to taste
2 tsp freshly ground black pepper, plus more to taste
½ tsp ground cumin
3 medium russet or Idaho potatoes, chopped into bite-size pieces
3 carrots, chopped into bite-size pieces
4 celery stalks, chopped
2 calabacitas or zucchini, chopped into bite-size pieces
½ bunch of fresh cilantro or mint, roughly chopped

For the tomato broth

5 Roma tomatoes
¼ white onion
2 garlic cloves
3 chipotle peppers in adobo sauce
1 tbsp chicken bouillon
1 tbsp tomato bouillon
½ tsp ground cumin
12 cups water or beef broth, divided
salt, to taste
freshly ground black pepper, to taste

For serving

Mexican rice
freshly squeezed lime juice
corn tortillas

1   In a large bowl, combine the ground beef, rice, eggs, onion, cilantro, garlic, chipotle pepper in adobo sauce, and spices. Mix until fully combined. Divide the meat into even-size balls (about the size of a golf ball) and set aside.

2   To make the broth, in a blender, combine the Roma tomatoes, onion, garlic cloves, chipotle peppers in adobo sauce, chicken bouillon, tomato bouillon, cumin, and 6 cups of water. Blend on high until smooth.

3   Transfer the broth mixture to a Dutch oven or stock pot over medium heat. Add the remaining 6 cups of water. Season to taste with salt and pepper. Bring to a simmer.

4   Add the meatballs and gently mix to submerge them in the broth. Cook for 20 minutes.

5   Add the potatoes, carrots, and celery. Cook covered for 10 minutes more.

6   Add the calabacitas and cilantro. Cook for 5 minutes more or until all vegetables are soft.

7   Serve with Mexican rice, lime juice, salsa de molcajete, and corn tortillas.

Ingredients

10 cups water, divided

4lb (1.8kg) raw shrimp, cleaned and deveined (reserve the shells)

3 medium golden, russet, or Idaho potatoes, cubed

3 carrots, cubed

1 chayote (mirliton), cubed

1 sprig of epazote leaves

2 bay leaves

1 calabacita, cubed

4 celery stalks, chopped

8oz (27g) canned baby corn

2 chipotle peppers in adobo sauce, chopped

½ bunch of fresh cilantro, chopped

For the soup base

2 tbsp vegetable oil

½ white onion, sliced

3 garlic cloves

3 Roma tomatoes, halved

5 New Mexico peppers or guajillo peppers, cleaned and deveined

2–4 chile de árbol peppers

1 cup hot water

7oz (199g) El Pato tomato sauce

2 tbsp ground dried shrimp

1 tsp whole peppercorns

1 tsp Mexican oregano

2 tsp vegetable, shrimp, or chicken bouillon

salt, to taste

For serving

freshly squeezed lime juice

sliced avocado

hot sauce (Tapatío or Valentina)

tostadas

tortilla chips

Tip

Omit the chile de árbol peppers and chipotle peppers if you prefer a milder soup.

Caldo de Camarón

Shrimp Soup

✦ **Makes** 8 servings   ✦ **Ready in** 1 hour

This soup is very hearty and delicious. The broth, shrimp, and vegetables form the perfect combination of flavors to enjoy year-round! My mom usually prepares this soup during Lent season, but it can be enjoyed during a cold, rainy day to warm up any heart. The best part about this soup is that if you're a big seafood lover, fish and shellfish can be added to maximize the flavor.

1   Make the soup base. In a medium frying pan over medium heat, heat the vegetable oil. Once hot, add the onion and garlic. Sauté for 2 minutes. Add the tomatoes facedown, and once they soften, flip them. Add the New Mexico and árbol peppers, frying each side for 10 seconds. Turn off the heat and add the hot water. Cover and let sit for 5 minutes.

2   Transfer the mixture to a blender. Add the tomato sauce, dried shrimp, whole peppers, oregano, vegetable bouillon, salt, and 4 cups of water. Blend on high until smooth.

3   In a Dutch oven over medium heat, combine the tomato mixture, shrimp shells, and the remaining 6 cups of water. Cook for 20 minutes.

4   Discard the shells and taste the broth. Add more salt if needed.

5   Add the potatoes, carrots, chayote, epazote leaves, and bay leaves. Cover and cook for 15 minutes more.

6   Add the calabacita, celery, baby corn, chipotle peppers in adobo sauce, and cilantro. Cook for 7 minutes more.

7   Add the raw shrimp and cook for 3 minutes more or until the shrimp is fully cooked. Discard the epazote and bay leaves.

8   Serve in bowls topped with freshly squeezed lime juice, avocado slices, and Tapatío hot sauce. Enjoy with tostadas or tortilla chips.

Ingredients

4lb (1.8kg) chicken drumsticks
2 tsp salt, or to taste
freshly ground black pepper,
    to taste
2 tbsp olive oil
1 white onion, halved, divided
10 cups hot water
3 Roma tomatoes
1 garlic clove
½ cup tomato sauce
1 tbsp chicken bouillon
1 tsp ground cumin
1½ cup uncooked white rice,
    rinsed
1 handful of fresh cilantro,
    roughly chopped

For serving

freshly squeezed lime juice
salsa of choice
corn tortillas

Caldo de Pollo con Arroz

Chicken and Rice Soup

✦ **Makes** 8 servings ✦ **Ready in** 55 minutes

When I was growing up, this soup was my grandma's remedy to cure any cold. Any time my kids are sick, they know just what to expect from me. It's quick, easy, and so simple that the whole family will enjoy it! Add vegetables or keep it simple. Either way, soup doesn't get more delicious or nourishing than this.

1   Clean the chicken and pat it dry with paper towels. Season with salt and pepper to taste.

2   In a large Dutch oven over medium-high heat, heat the olive oil and sear each piece of chicken for 2 minutes on each side.

3   Add half the onion and all the hot water. Bring to a boil. Use a strainer to remove any foam or scum that rises to the top of the broth.

4   Cover, reduce the heat to medium, and cook for 20 minutes. Scoop out 2 cups of broth and set aside. Discard the onion.

5   In a blender, combine the remaining half onion, tomatoes, garlic, tomato sauce, chicken bouillon, cumin, and the 2 cups of chicken broth. Blend until smooth.

6   Add the mixture and the rice to the chicken. Mix and cook, covered, for 20 minutes more. Add the cilantro and cook for 5 minutes more.

7   Serve with freshly squeezed lime juice, salsa, and corn tortillas.

Ingredients

5 quarts (4.7 L) water
1 white onion, whole
1 head of garlic
4 tbsp coarse salt, plus more
2lb (907g) bone-in beef ribs
2lb (907g) beef shank
2lb (907g) beef chuck roast, cut into bite-size pieces
3 Roma tomatoes, cubed
1 tbsp beef bouillon
1 tbsp tomato bouillon
2 chayotes (choko), cut into small pieces
1lb (454g) baby carrots or 5 large carrots cut into small pieces
5 ears of corn, cut into 2½-inch (6.4 cm) pieces
5 golden potatoes, cut into large chunks
2 calabacitas, cut into large chunks
1 bunch of fresh cilantro, roughly chopped
1 whole cabbage, quartered

For serving

corn tortillas
freshly squeezed lime juice
Salsa Macha (page **94**)

Caldo de Res

Hearty Beef and Vegetable Soup

〜〜〜〜〜〜〜〜〜〜〜〜

◆ **Makes** 8–10 servings
◆ **Ready in** 2 hours and 30 minutes

〜〜〜〜〜〜〜〜〜〜〜〜

This is the first soup I learned to make. I remember my mom giving me the instructions while she was at work. I felt so accomplished when my parents told me how delicious it was. I was intimidated at first, thinking this dish is complicated, but it's by far the easiest soup recipe you can ever make.

1   In a large stock pot over medium-high heat, combine the water, onion, garlic, and salt. Bring to a boil.

2   Add the three kinds of beef and return to a boil. Use a strainer to remove any foam or scum that rises to the top of the broth. Cover, reduce the heat to medium-low, and cook for 1 hour.

3   Transfer the garlic to a cutting board and use the side of a large knife to smash it. Return the garlic to the pot. Stir in the tomatoes, beef bouillon, and tomato bouillon. Taste and add salt as needed. Cover and cook for 55 minutes.

4   Add the chayotes, carrots, corn, and potatoes. Cook for 15 minutes.

5   Add the calabacitas and cilantro. Cook for 5 minutes more.

6   Add the cabbage and cook for 5 minutes more.

7   Serve with corn tortillas and the suggested toppings, or your favorites.

Ingredients

4 Roma tomatoes, roasted

4–8 serrano peppers, roasted

2 green hatch peppers or Anaheim peppers

¼ white onion, roasted

2 garlic cloves, roasted

1 handful of fresh cilantro, roughly chopped

salt, to taste

1 cup water

1½ tsp freshly ground black pepper

1½ tsp garlic salt

2 tbsp vegetable oil

3lb (1.4kg) beef steak or stew beef, cubed

3 russet potatoes, cubed

For serving

Mexican rice

queso fresco

Guacamole (page 90)

flour tortillas

Carne con Chiles y Papas

Beef Chili with Potatoes

✦ **Makes** 6 servings ✦ **Ready in** 45 minutes

This dish is the easiest and most delicious meal you can ever make. It will give you all the comfort and flavors of Mexico, but the best part is you can adjust the ingredients to your liking—from using your favorite cut of meat, beef, or pork to the spice level you want. This meal is one your whole family will love!

1 In a blender, combine the tomatoes, serrano peppers, hatch peppers, onion, garlic cloves, cilantro, salt, and water. Blend on high until smooth. Set aside.

2 Pat the meat dry with paper towels and season with salt to taste, pepper, and garlic salt.

3 In a Dutch oven over medium-high heat, heat the vegetable oil. Once hot, add the meat and brown it on all sides. Reduce the heat to medium-low and allow the meat to let out its own juices. Cover and allow the juices to evaporate, about 10 minutes.

4 Uncover and add the potatoes and the tomato and pepper mixture. Add a little more water (about ¼ cup), mix, and allow to simmer. Taste and add more salt as needed. Cover and cook for 15–20 minutes more or until the meat and potatoes are tender.

5 Serve with rice and the suggested toppings, or use your favorites.

Sopa de Conchitas con Pollo

Shell and Chicken Soup

~~~~~~

◆ **Makes** 8 servings   ◆ **Ready in** 1 hour

~~~~~~

On days when I don't feel like cooking or I don't know what to make, this recipe is my hero! You can never go wrong with a bowl of soup brimming with chicken and vegetables. It's best to eat this soup while hot because the pasta shells will quickly absorb the broth and you won't have as much soup to enjoy.

1   In a large pot over high heat, bring the water to a boil. Add ½ the onion, 1 head of garlic, oregano, bay leaves, salt, 1 tablespoon of pepper, and chicken breasts. Return to a boil. Use a strainer to remove any foam or scum that rises to the top of the broth. Lower the heat to medium, cover, and cook for 20 minutes.

2   Turn off the heat. Transfer the chicken to a cutting board and shred the meat. Strain and reserve the broth. Discard the strainer contents.

3   In a blender, combine the tomatoes, chipotle peppers, chicken bouillon, tomato bouillon, cumin, 2 cups of broth, the remaining ½ of onion, the remaining 2 garlic cloves, and the remaining 1 teaspoon of pepper. Blend on high until smooth. Set aside.

4   In a large pot over medium-high heat, heat the vegetable oil. Once hot, add the pasta shells and fry for 5 minutes.

5   Add the carrots, celery, and potatoes. Cook until the shells are fully golden brown, about 5–7 minutes.

6   Add the shredded chicken and cook for 2 minutes. Stir in the tomato mixture and the remaining strained broth. Bring to a simmer. Taste and add salt as needed.

7   Reduce the heat to medium and add the cilantro. Cover and cook for 15 minutes more.

8   Serve with fried taquitos and the suggested toppings, or use your favorite toppings of choice.

Ingredients

3 quarts (2.8 L) water
1 white onion, divided
1 head of garlic plus 2 garlic cloves, divided
fresh oregano, whole with stems
2 bay leaves
3 tbsp salt, to taste, plus more
1 tbsp plus 1 tsp freshly ground black pepper, divided
2lb (907g) bone-in chicken breasts
5 Roma tomatoes
2 chipotle peppers in adobo sauce
2 tsp chicken bouillon
1 tsp tomato bouillon
½ tsp ground cumin
¼ cup vegetable oil
1lb (454g) pasta shells
2 carrots, chopped into small cubes
2 celery stalks, chopped into small cubes
1 medium russet potato, cubed
½ bunch of fresh cilantro, chopped

For serving

fried taquitos
freshly squeezed lime juice
hot sauce (Tapatío or Valentina)
queso fresco
chopped avocados

Ingredients

2½lb (1.1kg) chuck tender roast, cut into large chunks
½ head of garlic plus 3 garlic cloves, divided
½ white onion
salt, to taste
1 tbsp beef bouillon
1 tbsp freshly ground black pepper
2 bay leaves
10 New Mexico peppers, cleaned and deveined
5 chile de árbol peppers (optional)
2 tsp New Mexico chili powder
1 tsp dried oregano
½ tsp cumin seeds
3 tbsp vegetable oil
3 tbsp all-purpose flour

For serving

Mexican rice
tostadas
flour tortillas

Chile Colorado

Red Beef Chili

✦ **Makes** 6–8 servings   ✦ **Ready in** 5 hours

You can make this chili in many ways—from using shredded meat, cubed meat, russet potatoes, and nopales to enjoying it in a burrito, on fry bread, or in a gordita! No matter which way you choose to enjoy this dish, it's going to be the best because the sauce is so flavorful and the meat is tender.

1   To a large pot, add the meat, the head of garlic, onion, and salt. Cover with water and bring to a boil. Use a strainer to remove any foam or scum that rises to the top of the broth.

2   Add the beef bouillon, black pepper, and bay leaves. Reduce the heat to medium-low, cover, and cook for 3–4 hours or until the meat is tender. Once done, transfer the beef to a cutting board and shred it. Discard the onion and garlic. Reserve the bay leaves.

3   Add the New Mexico peppers and the chile de árbol peppers (if using) to the pot and allow to soak for 5 minutes.

4   Transfer all the peppers to a blender. Add the chili powder, oregano, cumin seeds, 2½ cups of broth, and the remaining 3 garlic cloves. Blend on high until smooth.

5   In large frying pan over medium heat, heat the vegetable oil. Once hot, stir in the flour to create a roux. Add the chile sauce, straining as needed. Stir as you add the sauce to dissolve any clumps. Reduce the heat to low and bring to simmer. Taste and add salt as needed.

6   Return the shredded meat to the pot and make sure it's covered with sauce. Add the reserved bay leaves, cover, and cook for 5 minutes. Remove the bay leaves.

7   Serve with a side of rice and in burritos, tacos, tortas, tostadas, or gorditas or on fry bread—or any way you choose.

Ingredients

½ cup all-purpose flour

6 tsp salt, plus more to taste

1 tbsp plus 1 tsp freshly ground black pepper, divided

4lb (1.8kg) pork shoulder or chuck roast, cut into bite-sized pieces

10 Anaheim peppers or green hatch peppers, roasted and peeled

2–5 serrano peppers, roasted and peeled

1 white onion, divided (½ roasted and ½ chopped)

5 garlic cloves

½ bunch of fresh cilantro, chopped

3 cups chicken or beef broth

1½ tsp ground cumin

1 tbsp chicken bouillon

4 tbsp vegetable oil, plus more

5 Roma tomatoes, chopped

1½ tsp dried oregano

2 bay leaves

For serving

flour tortillas

Mexican rice

refried beans

Chile Verde

Slow Cooked Green Chili

◆ **Makes** 8 servings   ◆ **Ready in** 3 hours

Like chile rojo, chile verde can be made in many ways—from using shredded or cubed meat and russet potatoes to enjoying it in a burrito, enchilada, taco, or gordita or with rice and beans. Whichever way you choose to have this dish, this is going to be the best chili you've had because the sauce is flavorful and the meat is super tender.

1   On a large plate, combine the flour, salt, and 1 tablespoon of pepper. Dredge each piece of meat in this mixture and set aside.

2   In a blender, combine the Anaheim peppers, serrano peppers, roasted onion, garlic, cilantro, chicken broth, cumin, chicken bouillon, and the remaining 1 teaspoon of black pepper. Pulse until everything is crushed. Set aside.

3   In a large pot over high heat, heat the vegetable oil. Once hot, working in batches, add the coated meat in a single layer and sear until browned on all sides, about 16 minutes. Add more oil as needed during the cooking process to keep the meat from sticking to the pot. Transfer the meat to a large bowl. Set aside.

4   Add the chopped onion to the pot and sauté for 2 minutes. Add the tomatoes, pepper mixture, and oregano. Taste and add salt as needed.

5   Return the meat to the pot and bring to a simmer. Reduce the heat to the lowest setting and add the bay leaves. Cover and allow to cook for 1½–2 hours or until the meat is tender. Remove the bay leaves.

6   Serve with flour tortillas as well as Mexican red rice and beans.

Ingredients

5lb (2.3kg) beef honeycomb tripe

2lb (907g) beef feet

¾ cup freshly squeezed lime juice (about 6 limes)

5 quarts (4.7 L) plus 4 cups of water, divided, plus more

3 tbsp salt

1 white onion, quartered

1 head of garlic plus 4 garlic cloves, divided

3 bay leaves

2 tbsp menudo spice mix or dried oregano, divided

20 New Mexico peppers

4 ancho peppers or pasilla peppers

13 cups precooked hominy, rinsed, divided

For serving

Pan Bolillo (page 76)

freshly squeezed lime juice

red pepper chili flakes

chopped fresh oregano

chopped fresh cilantro

Menudo

Red Pepper Tripe Stew

◆ **Makes** 12 servings   ◆ **Ready in** 6 hours

Making menudo is a must—and the best menudo is made at home! To be honest, I don't think any store-bought menudo will ever come close to this one right here. The most important part of this recipe is the cleaning process for the tripe because a good menudo can smell like the butcher's shop. Using limes will help the acid eliminate any smells.

1   Rinse the tripe and beef feet with water until the water runs clear. Cut the tripe into about 1- to 2-inch (2.5–5 cm) pieces.

2   Place the tripe and beef feet in a large glass bowl and stir in the lime juice. Cover the rest with clean water. Cover the bowl with plastic wrap and allow to sit for at least 2 hours.

3   In a large stock pot over high heat, combine the 5 quarts (4.7 L) of water, salt, onion, the head of garlic, and bay leaves. Bring to a simmer.

4   Rinse the tripe and beef feet with water again until the water runs clear. Add the tripe and beef feet to the pot. Bring to a boil. Use a strainer to remove any foam or scum that rises to the top of the broth. Reduce the heat to medium and add 1 tablespoon of menudo mix. Cover and cook for 2 hours.

5   In a small saucepan over medium-high heat, cover the New Mexico and ancho peppers with water and bring to a boil.

6   In a blender, combine the peppers, 1 cup of hominy, the remaining 4 cups of water, and the remaining 4 garlic cloves. Blend on high until smooth.

7   Remove and discard the onion and the head of garlic from the pot. Stir in the pepper sauce (straining as needed), ancho peppers, the remaining 12 cups of hominy, and the remaining 1 tablespoon of menudo mix. Taste and add salt as needed. Cook for 30 minutes more or until the tripe and beef feet are tender.

8   Serve with buttered bolillo bread and the suggested toppings, or use your favorites.

Ingredients

5 quarts (4.7 L) water
½ white onion
1 head of garlic
4 bay leaves
3½ tbsp salt, plus more
3lb (1.4kg) bone-in chicken breasts
2lb (907g) chicken drumsticks
13 cups precooked hominy
2 tbsp vegetable oil
2 tbsp dried oregano

For the salsa

14 tomatillos, boiled
½ white onion, roasted
4 garlic cloves
1 tsp whole peppercorns
1 tsp cumin seeds
1 tsp dried oregano
½ tsp dried thyme
½ tsp dried marjoram
5 green hatch peppers, roasted, peeled, and deveined
1–5 serrano peppers, roasted and deveined
½ bunch of fresh cilantro, rinsed and chopped
5 romaine lettuce leaves, rinsed and chopped
3oz (11g) spinach leaves, rinsed and chopped
radish leaves, rinsed and chopped
2 tbsp chicken bouillon

For serving

tortilla chips
tostadas
freshly squeezed lime juice
finely shredded cabbage
sliced radishes
chopped fresh cilantro
chopped serrano peppers
avocado slices

Pozole Verde de Pollo

Green Chicken Soup

✦ **Makes** 8 servings   ✦ **Ready in** 50 minutes

This recipe is seriously the most delicious pozole verde ever—the chicken is so tender and the broth is so flavorful and bright. The best part is you can add as many greens as you want, which helps intensify the beautiful bright green of the broth! This is my kids' absolute favorite stew and I believe it's as healthy and nutritious as it can be. If you'd like it a little spicier, simply add more serrano peppers, but if you don't like spicy, use 1 to 2 jalapeños instead.

1   In a large stock pot over medium-high heat, combine the water, onion, garlic, bay leaves, and salt. Bring to a boil.

2   Add the chicken and return to a boil. Use a strainer to remove any foam or scum that rises to the top of the broth.

3   Add the hominy. Reduce the heat to medium-low and cook for 20 minutes.

4   Remove and discard the garlic and onion. Transfer the chicken breasts and drumsticks to a cutting board and shred the breasts. Strain 2 cups of chicken broth.

5   In a blender, make the sauce by combining the tomatillos, onion, garlic cloves, peppercorns, cumin seeds, oregano, thyme, and marjoram. Blend on high until smooth.

6   Add the hatch peppers, serrano peppers, cilantro, romaine lettuce, spinach, radish leaves, chicken bouillon, and the 2 cups of broth. Blend on high until smooth.

7   In a frying pan over medium heat, heat the vegetable oil. Once hot, add the tomatillo sauce and bring to a simmer.

8   Transfer the sauce to the pot and stir in the shredded chicken and drumsticks. Taste and add salt as needed. Simmer for 15 minutes.

9   Serve with tortilla chips or tostadas and the suggested toppings, or use your favorites.

Mole de Olla

*Hearty Beef and Vegetable Soup
in Guajillo Sauce*

◆ **Makes** 8 servings   ◆ **Ready in** 2½ hours

Ingredients

5 quarts (4.7 L) plus 2½ cups water, divided

1½ white onion, divided (1 quartered and ½ whole)

1 head of garlic plus 6 garlic cloves, divided

3 bay leaves

4lb (1.8kg) beef pot roast, cut into 2-inch (5 cm) cubes

2lb (907g) beef shank or chuck

4 tbsp salt, or to taste

4 tbsp vegetable oil

4 Roma tomatoes, halved

10 guajillo peppers, cleaned and deveined

5 ancho peppers or pasilla peppers, cleaned and deveined

1 bunch of epazote

1 tbsp beef bouillon

1 tbsp dried oregano

3 ears of corn, cut into 3-inch (7.6 cm) pieces

2 chayotes, cubed

½lb (227g) fresh green beans

5 large carrots, cut into 2-inch (5 cm) pieces

4 russet potatoes, peeled and cut into large cubes

2 calabacitas, cut into 1-inch (2.5 cm) pieces

For serving

freshly squeezed lime juice

chopped serrano peppers

chopped avocados

This soup is basically **Caldo de Res** (page 114) but in a delicious red guajillo sauce. This recipe is perfect if you like more flavor in your caldo de res soup. It's hearty—and the best part is you get to add all your favorite vegetables! I hope you and your loved ones enjoy this version as much as my friends and family do.

1   In a large pot over high heat, bring the 5 quarts of water to a boil. Add the 1 quartered onion, head of garlic, bay leaves, beef pot roast, beef shank, and salt. Return to a boil. Use a strainer to remove any foam or scum that rises to the top of the broth. Reduce the heat to medium-low, cover, and cook for 1 hour.

2   In a frying pan over medium heat, heat the vegetable oil. Once hot, add the tomatoes, the whole ½ onion, and the remaining 6 garlic cloves. Fry for 3 minutes. Add the guajillo peppers and ancho peppers. Fry for 1 minute more or until softened.

3   Transfer the tomato mixture to a blender. Add the epazote, beef bouillon, and the remaining 2½ cups of water. Blend on high until smooth.

4   Transfer the sauce to the frying pan (straining as needed) and stir in the oregano. Bring to a simmer.

5   Remove and discard the onion and the head of garlic from the pot. Stir in the tomato sauce. Taste and add salt as needed. Cook for 50 minutes.

6   Add the corn, chayotes, green beans, carrots, and potatoes, and cook for 15 minutes more.

7   Add the calabacitas and cook for 5 minutes more or until the vegetables are soft.

8   Serve with corn tortillas and the suggested toppings, or use your favorites.

Pozole Rojo

Red Pork Soup

✦ **Makes** 12 servings   ✦ **Ready in** 2 hours and 20 minutes

Pozole and **Menudo** (page 122) are similar yet unique in their own way. While menudo has a thick broth made with beef, pozole is usually made with pork but can also be made with chicken. If you're new to making Mexican cuisine, this is the perfect recipe to start with. If you don't like a lot of spice, replace the New Mexico peppers with guajillo peppers and don't add the chile de árbol peppers.

Ingredients

5 quarts (4.7 L) water

1½ white onion, divided (1 washed and quartered and ½ whole)

1 head of garlic plus 4 garlic cloves, divided

3 bay leaves

3 tbsp salt

4lb (1.8kg) pork shoulder roast, cut into large chunks

2lb (907g) neck bones or pork ribs

20 New Mexico peppers, cleaned and deveined

3 ancho peppers or pasilla peppers, cleaned and deveined

5 chile de árbol peppers

1 tbsp chicken bouillon

1 tsp ground cumin

1 tbsp vegetable oil

1 tbsp dried oregano

13 cups precooked hominy, rinsed

For serving

tostadas

finely shredded cabbage

chopped green onions

finely sliced radishes

freshly squeezed lime juice

chile de árbol salsa

1   In a large pot over medium-high heat, bring the water to a boil. Add the 1 quartered onion, head of garlic, bay leaves, salt, pork roast, and neck bones. Use a strainer to remove any foam or scum that rises to the top of the broth. Lower the heat to medium, cover, and cook for 90 minutes. Strain and reserve the broth. Set the roast and bones aside.

2   In a large saucepan over medium-high heat, combine the New Mexico peppers, ancho peppers, and chile de árbol peppers. Cover with water and bring to a boil.

3   Transfer all the peppers to a blender. Add the chicken bouillon, cumin, 4 cups of broth, the whole ½ onion, and the remaining 4 garlic cloves. Blend on high until smooth.

4   In a frying pan over medium heat, heat the vegetable oil. Once hot, add the pepper sauce (straining as needed) and bring to a simmer. Set aside.

5   Remove and discard the quartered onion and the head of garlic from the pot from step 1. Transfer the meat to a cutting board and shred it.

6   Add the pepper sauce and oregano to the remaining reserved broth. Return the meat to the pot. Add the hominy. Taste and add salt as needed. Cook for 30 minutes more.

7   Serve with tostadas and the suggested toppings, or use your favorites.

Ingredients

7 tbsp plus ¼ cup vegetable oil, divided
3 Roma tomatoes, halved
½ white onion, divided (¼ sliced and ¼ chopped)
2 garlic cloves
4 New Mexico peppers, cleaned and deveined
2 dried chipotle peppers
7 cups water, divided
1 tbsp chicken bouillon or beef bouillon
2 tsp tomato bouillon
½ tsp ground cumin
½ tsp freshly ground black pepper
1lb (454g) lean ground beef
salt, to taste
2 medium russet potatoes, cut into bite-size pieces
7oz (198g) uncooked fideo cut pasta (vermicelli)
1 handful of fresh cilantro leaves, chopped

For serving

cheese tacos (see Note)
tostadas
freshly squeezed lime juice
queso fresco
avocado slices

Note

To make the cheese tacos, simply add queso panela or shredded cheese and jalapeños to corn tortillas, roll them up, and fry them until golden brown.

Sopa de Fideo con Carne

Vermicelli Soup with Beef and Potatoes

◆ **Makes** 4–6 servings   ◆ **Ready in** 40 minutes

This sopita has to be my favorite! My mom would make this during the cold winter days and it just hits the spot. Now I make it for my kids. They ask for it year-round, not just when it's cold. I get to see the joy on their faces while blowing on the sopita and it brings back many childhood memories.

1   In a large frying pan over medium-high heat, heat 6 tablespoons of vegetable oil. Once hot, add the tomatoes and cook until they start to soften and break down, about 4 minutes.

2   Add the sliced onion and garlic cloves. Cook until the onion becomes translucent, about 3 minutes. Add the New Mexico peppers and chipotle peppers. Cook until softened, about 1 minute. Add 2 cups of water. Turn off the heat, cover, and allow to sit for 10 minutes.

3   Transfer the mixture to a blender. Add the chicken bouillon, tomato bouillon, cumin, and black pepper. Blend on high until smooth.

4   In a large pot over medium-high heat, heat 1 tablespoon of vegetable oil. Once hot, add the chopped onion and sauté for 2 minutes. Add the ground beef and salt. Brown the beef, then transfer it to a large bowl.

5   In the same large pot, heat the remaining ¼ cup of vegetable oil. Once hot, add the potatoes and cook for 4 minutes. Add the vermicelli and cook for 5 minutes, stirring to prevent the pasta from burning.

6   Stir the ground beef into the pot. Add the tomato broth and the remaining 5 cups of water. Bring to a simmer. Taste and add salt as needed.

7   Reduce the heat to the lowest setting and add the cilantro. Cover and cook for 15 minutes or until the potatoes have softened.

8   Serve with cheese tacos and the suggested toppings, or use your favorites.

Ingredients

4 quarts (3.8 L) water

1 white onion, quartered, divided

1 head of garlic plus 3 garlic cloves, divided

3 bay leaves

3lb (1.4kg) bone-in chicken breasts

1 bunch of fresh cilantro, roughly chopped

1 tbsp whole peppercorns

5 tbsp chicken bouillon

2 cups vegetable oil

20 corn tortillas, cut into strips

5 Roma tomatoes

5 New Mexico peppers

1 ancho pepper

1 tsp ground cumin

salt, to taste

1 (15.25oz [432g]) can sweet corn kernels, drained

1 (16oz [454g]) can pinto or black beans, drained

For serving

freshly squeezed lime juice

shredded Mexican cheese blend

sour cream

chopped serrano peppers

chopped and fried ancho peppers

thinly sliced avocado

Pico de Gallo (page 92)

queso fresco

Sopa Azteca

Chicken and Tortilla Soup

✦ **Makes** 6 servings   ✦ **Ready in** 50 minutes

This is a comforting meal, especially on cold days, with a flavor combination like no other. This isn't spicy at all—the chiles just add a good amount of flavor. But you can increase the heat by adding a few chipotle peppers or chile de árbol peppers. This soup is so delicious that even the pickiest eater will enjoy it!

1   In a large pot over high heat, bring the water to a boil. Add 3 onion quarters, 1 head of garlic, the bay leaves, and the chicken. Return to a boil. Use a strainer to remove any foam or scum that rises to the top of the broth.

2   Reduce the heat to medium. Stir in the cilantro, whole peppercorns, and chicken bouillon. Cover and cook for 25 minutes.

3   In a large frying pan over medium heat, heat the vegetable oil. Once hot, working in batches, add the tortilla strips and fry until golden brown, about 3–4 minutes. Set aside.

4   Transfer the chicken to a cutting board and shred it. Strain and reserve the broth.

5   Add the tomatoes and New Mexico peppers to the pot. Allow them to soften for 10 minutes.

6   In a blender, combine the tomatoes, peppers, 3 cups of broth, cumin, salt, the remaining 1 quarter of onion, and the remaining 3 garlic cloves. Blend on high until smooth. Set aside.

7   Return the chicken to the pot over medium heat. Stir in the tomato sauce and the remaining strained broth. Bring to a boil. Taste and add salt as needed.

8   Stir in the corn and beans. Bring to a boil, then remove the pot from the heat.

9   Serve with the tortilla strips and the suggested toppings, or use your favorites.

Breakfast Entrees

Chilaquiles Rojos..136

Chilaquiles Verde...138

Burritos para el Desayuno.......................................140

Huevos Encobijados..141

Huevos Rancheros...142

Huevos Ahogados...144

Chilaquiles Rojos

Red Chilaquiles

✦ **Makes** 4 servings   ✦ **Ready in** 30 minutes

Ingredients

12 New Mexico peppers or guajillo peppers, cleaned and deveined
1 Roma tomato
1 garlic clove
2 tsp salt
2 cups water, plus more for boiling
2 cups plus 2 tbsp vegetable oil, divided
20 corn tortillas, cut into triangles
½ white onion, sliced
10oz (284g) shredded Oaxaca cheese

For serving

fried eggs
crema Mexicana
queso fresco
avocado slices

Chilaquiles are super delicious and easy to make. Typically served with eggs to make a hearty breakfast, chilaquiles can also be served with rice and beans as an easy dinner. Any way or time of day, chilaquiles will hit the spot!

1   In a small pot over medium heat, combine the New Mexico peppers and tomato. Cover with water and allow to come to a boil.

2   Once boiling, transfer the peppers and tomato to a blender. Add the garlic, salt, and 2 cups of water. Blend on high until smooth. Set aside.

3   In a medium pan over medium heat, heat 2 cups vegetable oil. Once the oil is hot, add the tortilla triangles and fry for 2–3 minutes or until golden brown and crispy. Remove the chips from the pan and set aside.

4   In a large skillet over medium heat, heat 2 tablespoons vegetable oil. Once the oil is hot, add the onion slices and allow to fry for 2–3 minutes. Reduce the heat to low, add the sauce from the blender, and bring to a simmer. Once simmering, add the tortilla chips and coat with the sauce. Add the cheese and it allow to melt.

5   Serve with fried eggs, crema Mexicana, and queso fresco.

Ingredients

7 tomatillos, washed and
    peeled
6 serrano peppers
¼ white onion
1 garlic clove
salt, to taste
1 tsp freshly ground black
    pepper
1 handful of fresh cilantro,
    chopped
1 cup plus 1 tbsp vegetable oil,
    divided, for frying
15–20 corn tortillas, cut into
    triangles
10oz (284g) shredded Oaxaca
    cheese

For serving

fried eggs
crema Mexicana
queso fresco
chopped cilantro

Chilaquiles Verde

Green Chilaquiles

✦ **Makes** 4 servings   ✦ **Ready in** 30 minutes

This is one of my favorite dishes to make. I always seem to have the ingredients in my fridge. Typically served for breakfast with eggs, this recipe also works well as a lunch or dinner when served with chicken. Add fried eggs, top with cream, and garnish with cilantro for a beautiful presentation.

1   In a small pot over medium heat, combine the tomatillos, serrano peppers, and onion. Cover with water and bring to a boil.

2   Once boiling, transfer the tomatillos, serrano peppers, and onion to a blender. Add the garlic, salt, black pepper, and cilantro. Blend on high until smooth. Set aside.

3   In a medium pan over medium heat, heat 1 cup vegetable oil. Once the oil is hot, working in batches, add the tortilla triangles and fry for 2–3 minutes or until golden brown and crispy. Remove the chips from the pan and set aside.

4   In a medium skillet over medium heat, heat 1 tablespoon of vegetable oil. Once the oil is hot, add the sauce from the blender. Reduce the heat to low and bring to a simmer. Once simmering, add the tortilla chips and coat them with the sauce. Add the cheese and cover for 2–3 minutes to allow it to melt.

5   Serve with fried eggs, crema Mexicana, queso fresco, and chopped cilantro.

Ingredients

6oz (170g) bacon, chopped

½ white onion, chopped, divided

8oz (227g) chorizo

1½ cups cooked pinto beans, plus ¼ cup liquid

1–2 pickled jalapeño peppers, chopped

¼ cup pickled jalapeño juice

shredded cheese of choice, to taste

2 tbsp vegetable oil

1 Roma tomato, chopped

1 jalapeño pepper, chopped

8 whole eggs

salt, to taste

4 large flour tortillas

avocado slices, to taste (optional)

Burritos para el Desayuno

Breakfast Burrito

✦ **Makes** 4 burritos   ✦ **Ready in** 25 minutes

Who doesn't love breakfast? Why not spice up the most important meal of the day with this all-in-one burrito? Not only are the possibilities endless with this dish, but this can also be served as a sandwich, or you can cut the carbs completely and serve solo. In my opinion, this is the perfect way to start your day.

1   In a medium pan over medium heat, cook the bacon for 5 minutes. Add the chorizo and ¼ of the chopped onion. Cook for 5 minutes more.

2   Remove everything from the pan, but leave the bacon grease. Add the pinto beans. Heat and smash the beans. Add the pickled jalapeño juice and chopped jalapeños.

3   Return the bacon mixture to the pan and stir to combine. Remove the pan from the heat. After a few minutes, add the cheese and set aside.

4   In a separate medium pan, heat the oil. Add the Roma tomato, chopped jalapeño, and the remaining chopped onion. Cook until the onion is translucent. After a few minutes, add the eggs, season with salt, and scramble until the eggs are fully cooked.

5   Divide the meat and egg mixtures evenly among the tortillas. Add avocado slices (if using) to each tortilla. Roll the tortillas into burritos before serving.

Huevos Encobijados

Eggs in a Blanket

~~~~~~

✦ **Makes** 4 servings   ✦ **Ready in** 20 minutes

~~~~~~

When you feel like surprising your family for breakfast, this is the dish you want. Who doesn't want a tortilla stuffed with egg and covered in cheese and salsa? Get ready to amaze your family with this delicious, creative breakfast!

1   In a blender, combine the tomatoes, jalapeños, serrano pepper, chile de árbol, garlic cloves, onion, oregano, black pepper, and chicken bouillon. Blend on high until smooth.

2   In a medium frying pan over medium-high heat, heat the vegetable oil. Once hot, add the salsa from the blender. Let simmer for 5–7 minutes, then reduce the heat to low. Remove the pan from the heat and set aside.

3   Use a knife to cut a slit near the outer edge of a tortilla, forming a small pocket. Use your fingers to open the tortilla slit and carefully crack and add an egg to the inside of the tortilla. Place the tortilla into the sauce and cover with queso Oaxaca. Repeat with all the tortillas.

4   Once all the tortillas are filled and covered, place the lid on the pan and allow to cook for 5–7 minutes over medium-high heat.

5   Serve with refried beans.

Ingredients

6 Roma tomatoes, roasted
2 jalapeños, roasted
1 serrano pepper, roasted
2 chile de árbol peppers, toasted
2 garlic cloves, roasted
¼ white onion
½ tsp dried oregano
½ tsp freshly ground black pepper
2 tsp chicken bouillon
½ cup vegetable oil
salt, to taste
8 whole eggs
4 corn tortillas (see Tip)
2 cups shredded queso Oaxaca cheese

For serving
refried beans

Tip

~~~~~~~~~~~~~~~~~

When preparing the tortillas, be sure to allow the tortillas to puff up while cooking. When they puff and while they're hot, they're much easier to cut into to form the pocket needed for this recipe.

Ingredients

3 cups cooked pinto beans
8 corn tortillas
8 whole eggs

For the salsa ranchera

1 cup vegetable oil, divided
½ white onion, sliced
1 jalapeño pepper, sliced in
   strips
4 Roma tomatoes, cubed
1 tsp garlic salt
¼ tsp ground cumin
¼ tsp dried oregano
4oz (112g) hot tomato sauce
   (El Pato)
2 tbsp chopped fresh cilantro
   leaves
2 bay leaves

For serving

salsa ranchera
queso fresco
avocado slices
chopped cilantro

Huevos Rancheros

Mexican-Style Eggs

✦ **Makes** 4 servings   ✦ **Ready in** 20 minutes

A typical breakfast at the Regalado house consists of huevos rancheros. The salsa ranchera is what brings this delicious meal together. I like to serve this in a bean tostada and sometimes I'll add a layer of chorizo to spice things up a bit more. Regardless, this recipe is a favorite! You can just make the eggs and top them with the salsa ranchera served next to refried beans and enjoy with flour tortillas instead of the tostadas in this recipe.

1   Prepare the salsa ranchera. In a medium pan over medium-high heat, heat 2 tablespoons of vegetable oil. Once hot, add the onion and jalapeño. Sauté for 3 minutes.

2   Add the tomatoes, garlic salt, cumin, and oregano. Cook for 2 minutes more. The tomatoes should release their juices as you cook.

3   Stir in the tomato sauce and add the cilantro and bay leaves. Reduce the heat to the lowest setting and allow to simmer for 5 minutes more. Transfer the salsa ranchera to a medium bowl and discard the bay leaves.

4   In a medium pan over medium heat, add 2½ tablespoons vegetable oil. Add the beans, smash them down, and fry for a few minutes or until they're refried to your liking. Remove the pan from the heat and set aside.

5   In a small pan over medium low heat, heat the remaining vegetable oil. Once hot, add a tortilla and fry until golden brown, flipping until it's firm and crunchy. Transfer the tortilla to a kitchen towel. Repeat until all the tortillas have been fried into tostadas.

6   Reduce the heat to the lowest setting. In the same pan, cook the eggs to your liking, about 3–4 minutes.

7   To assemble, layer the beans, eggs, and salsa ranchera on each tortilla. Top the tostadas with additional salsa ranchera, queso fresco, avocado slices, and chopped cilantro.

Ingredients

4 Roma tomatoes, roasted
3 serrano peppers, roasted
¼ white onion, roasted
2 garlic cloves, roasted
4 chile de árbol peppers, slightly toasted
2 tbsp cilantro, chopped
½ tsp dried oregano
2 tsp salt
½ tsp freshly ground black pepper
2 tbsp vegetable oil, for frying
½lb (227g) longaniza or chorizo
10 whole eggs

For serving

Frijoles de la Olla (page 64)
queso fresco
chopped cilantro
sliced avocado

Huevos Ahogados

Drowned Eggs

✦ **Makes** 5 servings   ✦ **Ready in** 25 minutes

When you have a big family like mine and don't really feel like cooking but you want to make your family feel loved, this is the recipe for you! Whip up a quick salsa, mix it with longaniza (a Spanish sausage), crack in the eggs, and allow the steam to do its thing. This is a delicious, nearly effortless meal that will convince your family you've been in the kitchen for hours.

1   In a blender, combine the tomatoes, serrano peppers, onion, garlic cloves, chile de árbol peppers, cilantro, oregano, salt, and black pepper. Blend on high until smooth and set aside.

2   In a large skillet over medium-high heat, heat the vegetable oil. Once hot, add the longaniza, break it down, and cook for about 5 minutes.

3   Add the salsa from the blender, reduce the heat to medium-low, and bring to a simmer. Create a dip in the center of the mixture.

4   Crack the eggs into a ramekin or small bowl and then pour into the dip in the skillet mixture, cover, and allow to cook for 5–7 minutes or until they reach your desired doneness.

5   Serve immediately with **Frijoles de la Olla** (page 64) and garnish with queso fresco, chopped cilantro, and avocado slices—and enjoy the compliments!

Beef
Entrees

Barbacoa..148

Barbacoa de Res..150

Bistec Ranchero con Papas....................152

Taquitos Dorados de Carne Molida......154

Tacos de Deshebrada................................155

Carne Asada..156

Discada..158

Gorditas de Picadillo en Chile Verde......160

Ingredients

1-inch (2.5 cm) piece of cinnamon
4 avocado leaves, divided
4 bay leaves
6 whole cloves
10 whole allspice
1½ tbsp whole peppercorns
2 tsp dried oregano
2 tsp dried thyme
1 tsp dried marjoram
½ tsp coriander seeds
½ tsp cumin seeds
2 tbsp coarse salt
6lb (2.7kg) high fat content of beef (cheek, chuck roast, short ribs)
2 maguey or banana leaves, cleaned
1 white onion, halved, divided
12 garlic cloves, divided

For serving

tortillas
Salsa Roja (page 96)
Salsa Verde (page 98)
Mexican rice
refried beans
chopped fresh cilantro
chopped white onion
chile de árbol salsa
Salsa de Aguacate
   (page 100)
freshly squeezed lime juice

Barbacoa

Traditional Beef Barbacoa

✦ **Makes** 10–12 servings   ✦ **Ready in** 8 hours

Barbacoa is traditionally made from sheep or goat meat. It's slow cooked over an open fire or, more traditionally, in a hole dug in the ground and covered in maguey leaves. This barbacoa is unique: Slow cooked and made with a blend of spices, the secret is to also use a very fatty and tender cut of meat. This makes it so juicy.

1   In a small skillet over medium-low heat, combine the piece of cinnamon, 2 avocado leaves, and bay leaves. Toast until fragrant.

2   Once fragrant, add the whole cloves, whole allspice, whole peppercorns, oregano, thyme, marjoram, coriander seeds, and cumin seeds. Toast until fragrant, about 30 seconds.

3   Transfer everything to a blender or molcajete (or mortar and pestle) and crush well. Stir in the salt.

4   Pat the spice mix into the beef and rub firmly until the spices stick.

5   Transfer the beef to a large dish and cover with plastic wrap. Refrigerate overnight or for at least 4 hours. Remove the beef from the fridge at least 1 hour before cooking to bring it to room temperature.

6   Pass the maguey or banana leaves through fire to make them flexible. Their colors will change and they'll become shiny.

7   Assemble your steamer pot by adding water, ½ the onion, and 6 garlic cloves to the bottom. Cover the divider with the prepared leaves in a crisscross pattern. Use the longer sections of the leaves so you can fold them over to cover the meat.

8   Place the beef, the remaining 2 avocado leaves, the remaining ½ onion, and the remaining 6 garlic cloves in the steamer pot. Fold the banana leaves to cover the meat completely. Tightly cover the pot with aluminum foil and place the lid on the pot. Cook on medium-low heat for 4 hours or until the barbacoa easily pulls apart.

9   Allow to sit for 10–20 minutes before removing and shredding the beef. Discard the onion, garlic, and leaves.

10   Transfer the beef to a serving plate and stream the broth from the pot over the top.

11   Serve with Mexican rice and beans or as tacos with your preferred toppings.

Ingredients

4lb (1.8kg) beef chuck roast, cheek, shank, ribs, or any fatty meat, room temperature

5 tsp salt

1 tsp freshly ground black pepper

2 tbsp vegetable oil

1 white onion, quartered

4 bay leaves

For the adobo sauce

6–8 chipotle peppers in adobo sauce

5 garlic cloves

juice of 3 limes

¼ cup apple cider vinegar

2½ cups beef broth

1 tbsp ground cumin

1 tbsp beef bouillon

5 tsp New Mexico chili powder

2 tsp dried oregano

1½ tsp ancho chili powder

1 tsp salt

1 tsp whole peppercorns

½ tsp ground cloves or 6 whole cloves

Tip

You can also prepare this in the oven at 325°F (160°C) for 3 hours or in a crockpot on high heat for 4 hours.

Barbacoa de Res

Chipotle Beef Barbacoa

◆ **Makes** 8 servings   ◆ **Ready in** 3 hours

Barbacoa is traditionally made from sheep or goat meat and is slow cooked over an open fire or in a hole in the ground and covered in maguey leaves. This unique barbacoa is made with a spiced chipotle sauce in a multicooker. Oh how times have changed! Remember, you can substitute the meat as you please—just make sure it's high in fat.

1   Make the adobo sauce. In a blender, combine all the sauce ingredients. Blend on high until smooth and set aside.

2   Pat the beef dry with paper towels. Season with salt and black pepper, rubbing them in thoroughly.

3   Add the vegetable oil to a large multicooker and activate the sear setting. Working in batches, add the beef to the multicooker and cook for 4 minutes on each side. (See Tip.)

4   Once all the beef has been seared, cover it with the adobo sauce and add the onion and bay leaves. Close the lid, activate the sealing setting, cancel the sear setting, switch to the meat/stew setting, and cook for 70 minutes. (Settings might vary according to the cooker you're using.)

5   After cooking, allow the beef to rest for 15 minutes. Release the steam, open the multicooker, and remove the onion, bay leaves, and beef. Discard the onion and bay leaves.

6   Remove the fat (optional) and shred the beef. Return the beef to the multicooker to stay juicy until ready to serve. For serving options, see **Barbacoa** (page 148).

Ingredients

2 tbsp vegetable oil

1 small white onion, thinly sliced

1–2 jalapeño peppers or serrano peppers, sliced

2lb (907g) beef flank, thinly sliced

salt, to taste

2 tsp freshly ground black pepper

2 garlic cloves, minced

2 russet potatoes, peeled, cleaned, and cubed

4 Roma tomatoes, diced

7oz (200g) tomato hot sauce (El Pato)

¼ cup chopped fresh cilantro

2 bay leaves

For serving

refried beans

avocado slices

queso fresco slices

flour tortillas

Bistec Ranchero con Papas

Ranch Steak and Potatoes

✦ **Makes** 4–6 servings   ✦ **Ready in** 40 minutes

This dish brings back fond memories from my childhood. When my mom had to work and my dad was in charge, we knew we'd be eating this. I still ask him to make this easy, delicious recipe when I visit him. I like to serve this with a side of refried beans and flour tortillas. Very simple, very flavorful, very satisfying!

1   In a large, deep skillet over medium-high heat, heat the vegetable oil. Once hot, add the onion and sauté for 2 minutes. Add the jalapeño peppers and flank steak. Season with salt to taste and pepper. Add the garlic and allow the meat to brown.

2   Add the potatoes, cover, and cook for 5 minutes or until the juice from the meat has evaporated.

3   Stir in the tomatoes, tomato hot sauce, and cilantro. Taste for salt and adjust as needed. Reduce the heat to the lowest setting, add the bay leaves, cover again, and cook for 8 minutes or until the potatoes and meat are soft. Remove and discard the bay leaves.

4   Serve with a side of refried beans, avocado slices, queso fresco slices, and flour tortillas. Feel free to get creative with your own preferred toppings and sides.

Ingredients

3 small russet potatoes, rinsed

5 Roma tomatoes, divided (4 whole and 1 chopped)

4 jalapeño peppers

2 serrano peppers

1 white onion, halved, divided (½ whole and ½ chopped)

2 garlic cloves

salt, to taste

¼ cup fresh cilantro, chopped

1 tbsp plus 2 cups vegetable oil, divided

1lb (454g) lean ground beef

1 tsp garlic salt

1 tsp freshly ground black pepper

½ tsp ground cumin

20 corn tortillas

For serving

shredded lettuce

freshly squeezed lime juice

queso fresca

crema Mexicana

tomato slices

avocado slices

salsa (reserved)

Taquitos Dorados de Carne Molida

Ground Beef and Potato Taquitos

~~~~~~

✦ **Makes** 20 taquitos   ✦ **Ready in** 50 minutes

~~~~~~

I must admit, taquitos are and will always be my favorite dish. They're great for breakfast, lunch, or dinner. You can never go wrong with taquitos. This recipe is one of a few taquitos dorados dishes my mom used to make for the family. The best thing about this recipe is it's quick, easy, and satisfies even the fussiest eaters.

1   To a small pot over medium heat, add the potatoes and cover with water. Boil for 30 minutes or until fork-tender, then mash and set aside.

2   In a medium saucepan, combine the 4 whole tomatoes, jalapeño peppers, serrano peppers, and the 1 whole half of white onion. Cover with water and bring to a boil.

3   Transfer the saucepan mixture to a blender and add the garlic cloves and salt. Blend on high until everything breaks down. Add the cilantro and pulse 5 times until a salsa is achieved. Transfer to a medium bowl. Taste for salt and adjust as needed. Set aside for serving later.

4   In a large, deep frying pan over medium heat, heat 1 tablespoon of vegetable oil. Once hot, add the remaining chopped tomato and chopped onion. Sauté for 2 minutes. Add the ground beef, garlic salt, black pepper, and cumin. Break down the meat and cook for 7 minutes. Drain any oil, add the mashed potatoes, season with salt, and mix well.

5   In a separate large, deep frying pan over medium heat, heat the remaining 2 cups of vegetable oil.

6   Wrap 10 tortillas in a moist paper towel and microwave for 1 minute. Unstack the tortillas to prevent sticking and breaking. Repeat with the remaining 10 tortillas.

7   Spread 2 tablespoons of the meat and potato mixture onto a tortilla, keeping the spread about ½ inch (1.3 cm) away from the edges. Roll and repeat with the remaining tortillas.

8   Working in batches of 5 tortillas, place the tortillas seam down in the hot oil and fry for 2–4 minutes or until golden brown. Transfer the tortillas to a stack of dry paper towels, allowing the excess oil to drain.

9   Serve immediately with shredded lettuce, freshly squeezed lime juice, queso fresco, crema Mexicana, tomato slices, avocado slices, and salsa.

Tacos de Deshebrada

Shredded Beef Tacos

~~~~~~

◆ Makes 10 servings **◆ Ready in** 3 hours

~~~~~~

Easy, simple, delicious shredded beef tacos will please the whole family. The best thing is that you can make anything with leftover shredded beef from this recipe: burritos, tostadas, chimichangas—you name it!

1. In a large pot over medium-high heat filled halfway with water, combine the bay leaves, onion, and garlic. Bring to a boil. Once boiling, add the tender roast and short ribs. Return to a boil.

2. Use a strainer to remove any foam or scum that rises to the top of the broth. Reduce the heat to medium and add the salt, pepper, and cilantro to taste. Cover and allow to cook for 2–3 hours or until fork-tender.

3. Use tongs or a spoon to remove the meat from the pot and let it cool for 5–10 minutes. Once cooled, shred the meat. Discard the liquid in the pot.

4. In a medium skillet over medium-high heat, heat 3 tablespoons of vegetable oil. Once hot, add the red onion and Anaheim peppers. Sauté for 5 minutes. Once tender, add the shredded meat and cook for 5 minutes more. Add the tomatoes and cook for 10 minutes more. Remove the skillet from the heat.

5. Microwave the tortillas for about 45 seconds to make them pliable. Fill them with the shredded meat mixture and set aside.

6. Preheat the oven to the lowest temperature.

7. In a large skillet over medium-high heat, heat the remaining vegetable oil. Once hot, add the tacos 5–6 at a time and fry until golden on both sides. Be careful not to let the beef spill out. Keep the fried tacos on a baking sheet in the oven at the lowest temperature until all are fried.

8. Top with shredded cheese, shredded lettuce, freshly squeezed lime juice, and **Salsa Verde** (page 98) before serving.

Ingredients

3 bay leaves
1 white onion
1 head of garlic
2lb (907g) chuck tender roast, cut into chunks
2lb (907g) short ribs
salt, to taste
freshly ground black pepper, to taste
chopped fresh cilantro, to taste
3 cups vegetable oil, divided
1 red onion, sliced, to taste
3 Anaheim peppers, sliced
2 Roma tomatoes, chopped
30 corn tortillas

For serving

shredded cheese
shredded lettuce
freshly squeezed lime juice
Salsa Verde (page 98)

Ingredients

3lb (1.4kg) ranch, skirt, flank, or flap steak

For the marinade

¼ cup olive oil
juice of 4 limes
juice of 2 oranges
½ cup chopped fresh cilantro
½ white onion, sliced
1 jalapeño pepper, chopped
2 garlic cloves, minced
1½ tbsp salt or to taste
1 tbsp freshly ground black pepper
1 tbsp New Mexico chili powder
1½ tsp garlic powder
1½ tsp onion powder
1 tsp ground cumin
1 tsp dried oregano

Carne Asada

Marinated Steak

✦ **Makes** 8 servings   ✦ **Ready in** 5 hours

There's no party without some carne asada! Because it's made with a delicious marinade, everyone on your block won't be able to stop talking about your carne asada. Trust me, you aren't ready for how delicious this one is. You can serve carne asada as is with a side of rice and beans or as an excellent filling in tacos, quesadillas, tortas, gorditas, or burritos.

1   In a large bowl, combine all the marinade ingredients. Mix well.

2   Thinly slice the steaks and cover well with the marinade, cover, and refrigerate for a minimum of 4 hours.

3   Remove the steaks from the fridge and allow the meat to sit at room temperature for 1 hour.

4   In a large grill pan over high heat, cook the steak for 4–5 minutes on each side or until the desired doneness has been reached.

5   Allow to rest for 5 minutes before serving as desired.

Ingredients

1lb (454g) bacon, chopped

1½lb (680g) pork loin roast, cubed

2 tsp garlic salt

2 tsp freshly ground black pepper

½ tsp salt

1lb (454g) chuck steak, or choice, cubed

1lb (454g) lean ground beef

½lb (227g) chorizo

¾lb (340g) beef sausage, sliced

3 garlic cloves, minced

4 Roma tomatoes, chopped

1 small white onion, chopped

3 serrano pepper or jalapeño pepper, chopped

1 green hatch pepper or 2 chipotle peppers, chopped

½ cup hot tomato sauce (El Pato)

1 bunch of fresh cilantro

For serving

tortillas

freshly squeezed lime juice

Salsa Verde (page 98)

Discada

✦ **Makes** 10–12 servings ✦ **Ready in** 40 minutes

Discada has always been a family gathering favorite in my family. My tios used to gather around a large plow disc on the holidays while making this amazing dish. This recipe is the definition of versatile. You can include your favorite meats or veggies in many different combinations. You're probably wondering why this recipe is in the beef category when we're also cooking with pork—well, I had to put it somewhere!

1   To a large, deep skillet over medium-high heat, add the bacon and cook for about 5 minutes. Move the bacon away from the center and place the pork loin there. Season with garlic salt, salt, and black pepper. Cook for 15 minutes, rotating as the pork browns.

2   Move the pork loin away from the center. Add the cubed beef, ground beef, and chorizo to the center. Cook for 7 minutes, rotating as they brown.

3   Move the meats away from the center and add the beef sausage. Cook for 3 minutes, rotating as it browns.

4   Add the garlic, tomatoes, onion, serrano pepper, and green hatch pepper. Mix well and cook for 5 minutes or until the vegetables have softened. Stir in the hot tomato sauce and cilantro.

5   Serve as tacos with your preferred toppings.

Ingredients

2–5 serrano peppers or jalapeño peppers

5 tomatillos

1 Roma tomato

3 green hatch peppers or Anaheim peppers, roasted and peeled, divided

1 handful of fresh cilantro

½ small white onion, sliced, divided

1 garlic clove

salt, to taste

¼ cup water

2 tbsp plus 2 cups vegetable oil, divided

1lb (454g) lean ground beef

2 tsp garlic salt

1 tsp garlic powder

1 tsp dried oregano

1 tsp freshly ground black pepper

1 tsp onion powder

2 medium russet or Idaho potatoes, peeled, cleaned, and chopped into small cubes

For serving

shredded lettuce

creama Mexicana

queso fresco

tomato slices

avocado slices

Salsa Verde (page 98)

Gorditas de Picadillo en Chile Verde

Picadillo-Stuffed Gorditas

◆ **Makes** 12 gorditas ◆ **Ready in** 1 hour

These gorditas are a winner when you're craving something from a taco stand! But I always say homemade beats any restaurant or taco shop—and these gorditas prove that. The best way to enjoy these gorditas is to serve them immediately after they come out of the oil. They're hot and crunchy, and every bite is perfect. And the picadillo is so simple yet so flavorful. You can enjoy these all on their own or with your preferred toppings and sides.

1   In a medium saucepan over medium-high heat, combine the serrano peppers, tomatillos, and tomato. Cover with water and bring to a boil.

2   Once boiling, immediately transfer all the peppers, tomatillos, and tomato to a blender. Add 1 hatch pepper, cilantro, a small amount of sliced onion, garlic, salt, and water. Blend on high until smooth.

3   In a large skillet over medium-high heat, heat 2 tablespoons vegetable oil. Once hot, add the remaining onion slices and sauté for 2 minutes. Add the ground beef, garlic salt, garlic powder, oregano, black pepper, and onion powder. Break down the meat and allow to brown for about 3 minutes.

4   Add the potatoes and cook for 5 minutes more. Add the 2 remaining hatch peppers and mix. Add the green salsa from the blender and mix again. Bring to a simmer and taste for salt, adjusting as needed. Reduce the heat to the lowest setting, cover, and cook for 15 minutes.

5   In another large skillet over medium heat, heat 2 cups vegetable oil. Use the masa dough from **Masa para Tamales** (page 81), shape them, and fry until golden brown.

6   Remove the gorditas from the oil and cut a slit in the sides. Stuff with the meat filling. Repeat until all the gorditas are prepared.

7   Top with shredded lettuce, crema Mexicana, queso fresco, tomato slices, avocado slices, and **Salsa Verde** (page 98).

Chicken Entrees

Enchiladas Verdes con Pollo......................................164

Enmoladas con Pollo......................................166

Pollo Asado......................................168

Arroz con Pollo......................................170

Entomatadas con Pollo......................................171

Mole de Pollo......................................172

Tacos de Alambre......................................174

Taquitos Dorados de Pollo con Consommé............176

Tinga de Pollo......................................178

Tinga Verde de Pollo......................................180

Ingredients

4 cups water
1 white onion, halved, divided
4 garlic cloves, divided
salt, to taste
freshly ground black pepper, to taste
1lb (454g) chicken breasts
15 tomatillos
5 serrano peppers or jalapeño peppers
2 poblano peppers, charred, peeled, and deveined
2 Anaheim peppers, charred, peeled, and deveined
¼ cup chopped fresh cilantro
½ tsp ground cumin
1 tsp dried oregano
1 tsp chicken bouillon
1 cup vegetable oil
20 corn tortillas
10oz (284g) queso fresco, crumbled

For serving

shredded lettuce
15oz (425g) crema Mexicana
chopped fresh cilantro
chopped white onion
queso fresco, to taste

Tip

If you prefer a spicier dish, consider adding additional serrano peppers.

Enchiladas Verdes con Pollo

Green Chicken Enchiladas

✦ **Makes** 20 enchiladas   ✦ **Ready in** 45 minutes

If I had to pick one dish to eat for the rest of my life, I'd pick enchiladas—without a doubt. Enchiladas are very versatile—meat, no meat, it works either way. The green enchiladas here need to be on everyone's menu because they're seriously the most delicious. This recipe is so good, my kids are always asking for seconds!

1   In a medium saucepan over medium-high heat, combine the water, ½ onion, 2 garlic cloves, and salt and pepper to taste. Bring to a boil. Once boiling, add the chicken breasts, reduce the heat to medium, and cook for 20 minutes. Use a strainer to remove any foam or scum that rises to the top of the broth. Cook for 5 minutes more or until the chicken is cooked through. Remove the chicken from the pot and let rest for a few minutes before shredding. Reserve 2 cups of broth and set aside.

2   In a medium pot over medium heat, combine the tomatillos, serrano peppers, and the remaining ½ onion. Cover with water and bring to a boil.

3   Once boiling transfer the tomatillos, onion, and serrano pepper to a blender. Add poblano peppers, Anaheim peppers, cilantro, cumin, oregano, chicken bouillon, the remaining 2 garlic cloves, and the 2 cups of reserved chicken broth. Blend on high until smooth.

4   Transfer the sauce to a medium pot over medium-low heat, straining as needed. Taste for salt and adjust as needed. Simmer until the sauce thickens slightly, about 5–10 minutes. Stir 1 cup of sauce into the shredded chicken. Reserve the remaining sauce.

5   In a small deep skillet over medium heat, heat the vegetable oil. Once hot, use kitchen tongs to fry a tortilla until it blisters, about 10 seconds. Place between paper towels to remove excess oil. Repeat until all the tortillas have been fried.

6   One at a time, dip the tortillas in the sauce and fill with shredded chicken and queso fresco. Roll and place them seam side down on a serving plate. In threes, add a little more sauce over them and garnish with crema Mexicana, lettuce, more crema Mexicana, cilantro, onion, and queso fresco. Repeat until all the enchiladas have been prepared, then serve immediately.

Ingredients

4 quarts (3.8L) water

1½ white onions, divided (½ whole, ½ cut into strips, and ½ chopped)

½ head of garlic

2lb (907g) chicken breasts

salt, to taste

1 (3oz [90g]) Mexican hot chocolate (Abuelita or Ibarra)

¾ cup vegetable oil, divided, plus more

8 New Mexico peppers or guajillo peppers

2 garlic cloves

15 saltine crackers

1 Roma tomato, halved

½ tsp ground cinnamon

½ tsp ground cumin

8.25oz (233g) Doña Maria Mole (optional)

2lb (907g) queso fresco

24 corn tortillas

For serving

crema Mexicana

queso fresco

sliced red onion

chopped fresh cilantro

Mexican rice

refried beans

Enmoladas con Pollo

Mole Sauce Enchiladas with Chicken

◆ **Makes** 8 servings   ◆ **Ready in** 1 hour

If you like mole, then you're going to love this recipe! If you have leftover mole sauce, you'll have this recipe finished in 15 minutes. If not, don't worry—I'm here to show you how to make the most delicious mole sauce. My mole recipe is a little sweet yet a little spicy. If you're aiming for a sweet mole, use guajillo peppers.

1   In a large pot over medium-high heat, bring the water to a boil. Add the ½ onion, garlic, chicken breasts, and salt. Return to a boil and use a strainer to remove any foam or scum that rises to the top of the broth. Reduce the heat to medium, cover, and cook for 25 minutes.

2   Remove the chicken from the broth, shred, and set aside. Reserve 2 quarts (1.9L) of strained broth and add the chocolate tablet to it, allowing the tablet to dissolve completely.

3   In a medium frying pan over medium heat, heat 3 tablespoons of vegetable oil. Once hot, lightly fry the New Mexico peppers, about 10 seconds, then add them to the reserved chicken broth.

4   Fry the onion strips until translucent, then transfer them to the broth. Repeat the cooking and transfer process with the garlic cloves, crackers, and tomato, adding more oil as needed to cook them.

5   Transfer everything from the pot to a blender and add the cinnamon, cumin, and mole (if using). Blend on high until smooth.

6   In a deep frying pan, heat 1 tablespoon of vegetable oil. Once hot, add the mole sauce from the blender. Stir continuously and bring to a simmer. Taste for salt and adjust as needed. Reduce the heat to the lowest setting and simmer for 10 minutes, mixing continuously.

7   In a small bowl, combine the queso fresco and the remaining ½ chopped onion. Set aside.

8   In a small pan over medium heat, heat the remaining ½ cup of vegetable oil. Once hot, lightly fry a tortilla until it blisters, about 10 seconds. Repeat until all tortillas have been fried.

9   Dip a tortilla in the mole sauce and stuff with 2 tablespoons of shredded chicken and the cheese mixture.

10   Add mole sauce to a plate and place three enmoladas on top. Cover with more sauce and top with crema Mexicana, queso fresco, sliced red onion, and chopped cilantro before serving. Mexican rice and refried beans also make excellent sides.

Ingredients

7 garlic cloves

3 tbsp Chef Mérito chicken red seasoning (or chicken seasoning of choice)

2 tsp freshly ground black pepper

2 tsp ground cumin

1 tsp smoked paprika

1 tsp New Mexico chili powder

½ tsp ground cayenne

½ tsp salt

juice of 3 limes

½ cup water

½ cup freshly squeezed orange juice

½ cup pineapple juice

⅓ cup olive oil

1 small white onion, sliced

2 small jalapeño peppers, sliced

3lbs (1.4kg) chicken (breasts or thighs)

Pollo Asado

Marinated Grilled Chicken

◆ **Makes** 6–8 servings

◆ **Ready in** 4–5 hours

If you're hosting a party but have family and friends who don't like red meat, then prepare to surprise them with this delicious pollo asado! There's nothing above this delicious, marinated grilled chicken. It's perfect to enjoy at your next barbecue or really any day you find yourself craving chicken.

1   In a blender, combine the garlic, chicken seasoning, pepper, cumin, paprika, chili powder, cayenne, salt, lime juice, and water. Blend on high until smooth.

2   In a large bowl, combine the blender mixture, orange juice, pineapple juice, olive oil, onion, and jalapeño peppers. Mix well to create the marinade. Place the chicken in the bowl and coat with the marinade. Cover and refrigerate for a minimum of 3 hours. Remove the marinated chicken from the fridge at least 1 hour before cooking. Discard the marinade.

3   In a large skillet or grill over medium heat, cook the chicken for 7 minutes on each side or until the internal temperature reaches 170°F (77°C). Allow the chicken to rest for 5 minutes and slice before serving.

Ingredients

4 medium boneless chicken thighs

chicken seasoning of choice, to taste (Chef Merito recommended)

freshly ground black pepper, to taste

3 tbsp vegetable oil, divided

¼ red onion, chopped

1 red bell pepper, chopped

1 green bell pepper, chopped

2 garlic cloves, minced

2 Roma tomatoes, chopped

1 cup uncooked white rice

1½ cups chicken broth

2 tsp ground paprika

¼–½ tsp red pepper chili flakes

½ tsp ground turmeric

½ tsp ground cumin

1 tsp chicken bouillon

2 bay leaves

1 handful of fresh cilantro, chopped

Arroz con Pollo

Chicken and Rice

◆ **Makes** 4 servings   ◆ **Ready in** 35 minutes

Who doesn't love arroz con pollo? This quick and easy meal is so versatile and can be adjusted to suit any head count. Let's not forget to mention that all you need is one pot! Less dishes for the kids to clean after they devour this delicious meal.

1   Season the chicken thighs with chicken seasoning and black pepper.

2   In a medium skillet over medium-high heat, heat 1 tablespoon of vegetable oil. Once hot, add the chicken and cook for 3–4 minutes on each side. Remove the chicken and set aside.

3   In the same medium skillet, heat 1 tablespoon of vegetable oil. Once hot, add the onion and red and green bell peppers. Sauté for 2 minutes or until the onions have softened. Add the garlic and Roma tomatoes. Cook for 2 minutes more.

4   Add the remaining 1 tablespoon of vegetable oil and rice. Continuously stir the rice for an 4 minutes more or until fried. Stir in the chicken broth, paprika, chili flakes, turmeric, cumin, and chicken bouillon.

5   Return the chicken to the skillet and add the bay leaves. Cover with a lid and set on low heat. Simmer for 25–30 minutes or until the rice is tender.

6   Garnish with freshly chopped cilantro. Remove the bay leaves before serving.

Entomatadas con Pollo

Tomato Sauce Enchiladas with Chicken

✦ **Makes** 25 entomatadas ✦ **Ready in** 45 minutes

These tortillas dipped in a delicious tomato sauce and stuffed with chicken and cheese are one of my kids' favorites! This recipe mostly consists of tomatoes, but I like to add jalapeño peppers and chile de árbol peppers for a little kick and a little flavor. It's not spicy—using 10 tomatoes balances the spice out—but feel free to skip these additions if you prefer.

1   In a large pot over high heat, bring the water to a boil. Add 1 onion half, 6 garlic cloves, salt, and chicken. Bring to a simmer. Use a strainer to remove any foam or scum that rises to the top of the broth. Reduce the heat to medium, cover, and cook for 25 minutes.

2   Remove the chicken, onion, and garlic cloves. Discard the onion and garlic cloves. Shred the chicken and set aside.

3   In the same large pot, combine the remaining 1 onion half, tomatoes, jalapeño peppers, and chile de árbol peppers. Cook for 10 minutes more. Reserve ½ cup of broth and discard the rest of the broth.

4   Transfer the contents of the pot to a blender and add the oregano, chicken bouillon, bay leaves, the reserved ½ cup of broth, and the remaining 3 garlic cloves. Blend on high until smooth.

5   In a medium frying pan over medium heat, heat 1 tablespoon of vegetable oil. Once hot, add the sauce from the blender. Bring to a simmer and taste for salt, adjusting as needed. Simmer for 5 minutes. Set aside.

6   In a large skillet over medium heat, heat ½ cup of vegetable oil. Once hot, lightly fry a tortilla until it blisters, about 10 seconds. Repeat until all tortillas have been fried. Remove the oil from the pan.

7   In the same pan, heat 1 tablespoon of vegetable oil and fry the chopped ½ onion for 2 minutes. Stir in the shredded chicken and cook for 2 minutes more. Stir in ½ cup of the tomato sauce and set aside.

8   Dip a tortilla in the tomato sauce, add 2 tablespoons of chicken and queso fresco, fold in half, and repeat until all the entomatadas have been prepared.

9   Spread some tomato sauce on a plate, place the entomatadas on top, and top with more sauce, crema Mexicana, chopped cilantro, chopped white onion, queso fresco, and a few slices of tomato before serving. Rice and refried beans also make excellent sides.

Ingredients

4 quarts (3.8L) water
1½ white onions, divided (2 halves, plus ½ chopped)
9 garlic cloves, divided
salt, to taste
2lb (907g) chicken breasts with ribs
10 Roma tomatoes
3 jalapeño peppers
2 chile de árbol peppers
1½ tsp dried oregano
1 tbsp chicken bouillon
2 bay leaves
¾ cup vegetable oil, divided, plus more
2lb (907g) queso fresco, crumbled
25 corn tortillas

For serving

crema Mexicana
chopped fresh cilantro
chopped white onion
queso fresco
tomato slices
Mexican rice
refried beans

Ingredients

4 quarts (3.8L) water

2 white onions, divided (1 whole, ½ cut into strips, ½ chopped)

1 head of garlic

5lb (2.3kg) chicken, thighs or drumsticks

salt, to taste

½–1 (3oz [90g]–6oz [180g]) Mexican chocolate tablet (Abuelita or Ibarra)

4 tbsp vegetable oil, divided, plus more

8 New Mexico peppers or guajillo peppers, cleaned and deveined

1 pasilla pepper, cleaned and deveined

2 garlic cloves

15 saltine crackers

1 Roma tomato, halved

1-inch (2.5 cm) cinnamon stick

¼ tsp cumin seeds

1 tbsp toasted sesame seeds

4 whole allspice berries

8.25oz (233g) Mole Doña Maria (optional)

For serving

Mexican rice

Espagueti Rojo (page 70)

corn tortillas

toasted sesame seeds

Tip

For a sweeter mole, make sure to use guajillo peppers and extra chocolate.

Mole de Pollo

Chicken Mole

✦ **Makes** 8 servings   ✦ **Ready in** 1 hour

Welcome to the easiest, most delicious mole recipe you'll ever make—with fewer spices and fewer ingredients. My grandma made this recipe all the time, and while I tried my own variations on it, I always came back to this original recipe. It's just too good! Many people think mole is super complicated, but I'm happy to share just how easy it is. In Mexico, mole is served for special occasions, but this recipe can turn any meal into one.

1   In a large Dutch oven over medium-high heat, bring the water to a boil. Add 1 whole onion, head of garlic, chicken, and salt. Return to a boil and use a strainer to remove any foam or scum that rises to the top of the broth. Reduce the heat to medium, cover, and cook for 25 minutes.

2   Remove everything from the broth. Shred the chicken and set aside. Strain and reserve 2 quarts (1.9L) of broth. Discard the rest.

3   To the reserved broth, add the chocolate and allow it to dissolve.

4   In a medium saucepan over medium heat, heat 3 tablespoons of vegetable oil. Once hot, lightly fry the New Mexico peppers and pasilla pepper, about 10 seconds. Transfer to the reserved chicken broth.

5   Add the onion strips to the saucepan and cook until translucent. Transfer to the reserved broth. Repeat the cooking and transfer process with the garlic cloves, crackers, and tomato, adding more oil as needed to cook them.

6   Transfer everything except for the shredded chicken to a blender and add the cinnamon stick, cumin, sesame seeds, whole allspice, and mole (if using). Blend on high until smooth.

7   Dry the Dutch oven, return to medium-high heat, and heat the remaining 1 tablespoon of vegetable oil. Once hot, add the mole sauce from the blender. Stir continuously and bring to a simmer. Taste for salt and adjust as needed. Reduce the heat to the lowest setting and simmer for 10 minutes. Continue mixing until the sauce thickens.

8   Add the shredded chicken to the sauce and cook for 10 minutes until the chicken is hot. Reseason with salt as needed.

9   Serve with Mexican rice, **Espagueti Rojo** (page 70), and corn tortillas. Garnish with toasted sesame seeds before serving.

Ingredients

1½lb (680g) chicken breasts or other meat of choice, cubed

juice of 1 lemon

1 garlic clove, minced

1½ tsp salt or to taste

1 tsp freshly ground black pepper

1 tsp ground cumin

2 tsp onion powder

2 tsp chili powder

10 bacon strips, cut into ½-inch (1.3 cm) pieces

1 white onion, chopped

1 red bell pepper, chopped

1 green bell pepper, chopped

¼ cup chopped fresh cilantro

10oz (284g) shredded Oaxaca cheese

20–25 corn or flour tortillas

For serving

sour cream

Salsa de Aguacate (page 100)

Tacos de Alambre

Cheesy Fajita Tacos

~~~~~~

◆ **Makes** 6 servings
◆ **Ready in** 35 minutes

~~~~~~

This recipe is essentially grilled chicken topped with chopped bacon, bell peppers, onions, and cheese. Very similar to fajitas! The best part about this dish is it's fast and easy to put together, and it can be made with chicken, shrimp, beef, or anything you have handy. You can never go wrong with some tacos de alambre.

1   In a large bowl, combine the chicken breasts, lemon juice, garlic, salt, black pepper, cumin, onion powder, and chili powder. Mix until well combined.

2   In a large skillet over medium-high heat, cook the bacon for 5–8 minutes or until fully cooked. Remove the bacon from the skillet, leaving the oil behind.

3   Add the chicken to the bacon oil and cook for 8 minutes, stirring frequently. Remove the chicken and discard the oil.

4   Add the onion and red and green bell peppers to the skillet and sauté for 7 minutes. Reduce the heat to the lowest setting, stir the chicken into the vegetables, and taste for salt, adjusting as needed.

5   Stir in the cooked bacon and cilantro. Top with the cheese, cover, and cook until the cheese melts, about 5 minutes.

6   Serve in tortillas in equal portions. Top with sour cream and **Salsa de Aguacate** (page 100) before serving.

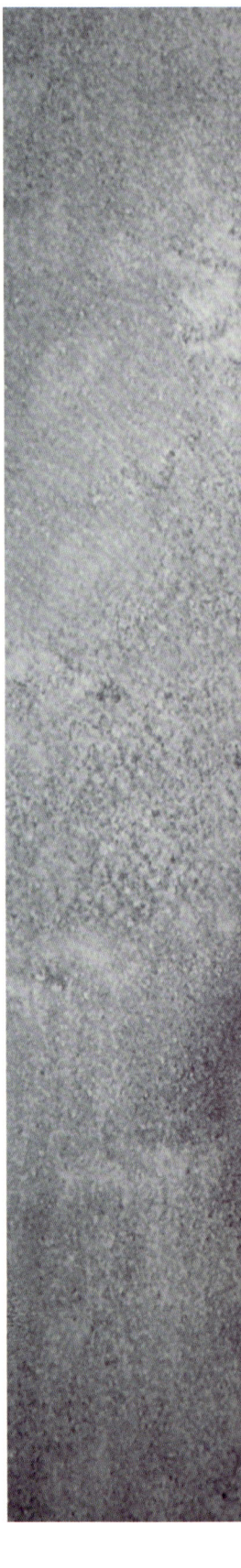

Ingredients
25–30 corn tortillas
2 cups plus 1 tbsp vegetable oil, divided

For the chicken and consommé broth
2 quarts (1.9L) water
½ white onion, whole
2 garlic cloves
2lb (907g) chicken breasts with ribs
1 tsp tomato bouillon
1 tsp chicken bouillon
salt, to taste
1 bunch of fresh cilantro

For the salsa
3 New Mexico peppers, cleaned and deveined
10–12 chile de árbol peppers, cleaned and deveined
5 Roma tomatoes, whole
1 tsp dried oregano
½ tsp freshly ground black pepper
½ tsp ground cumin

For the filling
¼ white onion, chopped
1 jalapeño pepper or serrano pepper, chopped
salt, to taste
1 Roma tomato, chopped

For serving
crema Mexicana
sour cream
queso cotija
shredded lettuce
queso fresco
freshly squeezed lime juice
tomato slices
avocado slices
½ cup consommé (reserved)

Taquitos Dorados de Pollo con Consommé

Drowned Chicken Taquitos

✦ **Makes** 25–30 taquitos   ✦ **Ready in** 1 hour and 10 minutes

These taquitos are a must when it's cold outside and you want something to warm you up. They're delicious on their own or drowned in the consommé made from a delicious red salsa.

1   Begin by preparing the chicken and consommé broth. In a large pot over medium-high heat, bring the water to a boil. Add the whole ½ onion, garlic cloves, and chicken breasts. Return to a boil and use a strainer to remove any foam or scum that rises to the top of the broth. Add the tomato bouillon, chicken bouillon, and salt. Reduce the heat to medium, add the cilantro, cover, and cook for 25 minutes. When the cooking is complete, remove the chicken breasts and cilantro. Discard the cilantro. Once the chicken has cooled some, shred and set aside.

2   Make the salsa. In a large skillet over medium heat, toast the New Mexico peppers and the chile de árbol peppers for about 5 minutes on each side.

3   Transfer the peppers to the broth in the pot and add the 5 whole Roma tomatoes. Cook for 5–10 minutes or until the tomatoes begin to open up.

4   Transfer the onion, garlic cloves, tomatoes, peppers, and 2 cups of broth to a blender. Add the oregano, black pepper, and cumin. Blend on high until a smooth salsa forms. Reserve 1½ cups of consommé and set aside. (This is an optional topping when serving.)

5   Strain 4 cups of consommé from the pot, discard the rest, and return the pot to medium heat. Return the 4 cups of consommé to the pot and add the salsa from the blender. Bring to a simmer and taste for salt, adjusting as needed.

6   Prepare the filling. In a medium frying pan over medium heat, heat 1 tablespoon of vegetable oil. Add the ¼ chopped onion and jalapeño pepper. Sauté for 2 minutes. Reseason with more salt, to taste. Add the shredded chicken and chopped tomato. Cook for 2 more minutes, then add 1 cup of the consommé.

7   Wrap 10 tortillas in a moist paper towel and microwave for 1 minute. Unstack the tortillas to prevent sticking and breaking. Repeat with the remaining tortillas.

8   Spread 2 tablespoons of the chicken mixture on a tortilla, keeping the spread about ½ inch (1.3 cm) away from the edges. Roll and repeat with the remaining tortillas.

9   In a large skillet, heat the remaining 2 cups of vegetable oil. Fry the tortillas seam side down in batches of 5 for 3–4 minutes or until golden brown. Remove from the oil and set aside on a stack of dry paper towels for 1 minute, allowing the excess oil to drain.

10 Serve in a bowl and top with drizzle of crema Mexicana or sour cream as well as queso cotija, shredded lettuce, queso fresco, freshly squeezed lime juice, tomato slices, avocado slices, and the reserved consommé.

Ingredients

2½ quarts (2.4L) water
½ white onion
3 garlic cloves
2 bay leaves
2lb (907g) chicken breasts
2 tbsp vegetable oil
salt, to taste

For the sauce

3 Roma tomatoes
¾ white onion, divided (¼ whole and ½ sliced)
¾ cup broth (reserved)
2 garlic cloves
6 chipotle peppers

For serving

tostadas
tortillas of choice
shredded lettuce
sour cream

Tinga de Pollo

Chicken Tinga

✦ **Makes** 6 servings ✦ **Ready in** 45 minutes

This original recipe is quite simple: shredded chicken in a spicy chipotle salsa. My kids adore this dish that's also perfect for any party or gathering. Just be prepared for everyone to want more! My favorite thing about this dish is that it works for everyone. You can serve it on tostadas, in tortillas, or really any way you prefer.

1   In a medium pot on medium heat, combine the water, onion, garlic, and bay leaves. Bring to a boil. Once boiling, add the chicken breasts and return to a boil. Once boiling again, use a strainer to remove any foam or scum that rises to the top of the broth. Reduce the heat to medium-low, cover, and cook for 20 minutes.

2   Transfer the cooked chicken to a bowl and allow it to cool. Use two forks to shred the cooled chicken and set it aside.

3   To make the sauce, add the tomatoes to the pot and cook for 5–7 minutes. Reserve ¾ cup of the broth and set aside.

4   In a blender, combine the tomatoes, ¼ whole onion, the reserved broth, garlic, and chipotle peppers. Blend on high until smooth.

5   In a large skillet over medium heat, heat the vegetable oil. Once hot, add the sliced onions and cook until translucent. Add the shredded chicken and cook for 3 minutes more. Add the sauce and simmer for 10 minutes until the chicken is hot.

6   Serve on tostadas or as quesadillas. Top with shredded lettuce and sour cream.

Tinga Verde de Pollo

Green Chicken Tinga

~~~~~~

◆ **Makes** 8 servings   ◆ **Ready in** 40 minutes

~~~~~~

Ingredients

3lb (1.4kg) chicken breasts

all-purpose seasoning of choice, to taste

3 tbsp vegetable oil

¾ white onion, sliced

1 poblano pepper, roasted, peeled, deveined, and sliced

For the sauce

12 tomatillos, boiled

3 whole poblano peppers, roasted, peeled, and deseeded

5 serrano peppers or jalapeño peppers, roasted, peeled, and deseeded

¼ white onion, roasted

3 garlic cloves

1 tbsp chicken bouillon

1 tsp salt

½ tsp whole peppercorns

¼ tsp whole cumin

¾ cup water

1 handful of fresh cilantro

For serving

tostadas

sour cream

shredded lettuce

crema Mexicana

queso fresco

Where there's tinga roja, there's also tinga verde—and let me tell you, it doesn't disappoint. The best way to enjoy this recipe is in a tostada topped with sour cream, shredded lettuce, crema Mexicana, and queso fresco. Very simple yet very flavorful!

1   Prepare the sauce. In a blender, combine the tomatillos, 3 whole poblano peppers, serrano peppers, ¼ roasted onion, garlic, chicken bouillon, salt, whole peppercorns, cumin, and water. Blend on high until smooth. After blending, add a handful of cilantro to the blender and pulse until chopped. Set aside.

2   Season the chicken breasts with all-purpose seasoning.

3   In a large skillet over medium-high heat, heat the vegetable oil. Once hot, add the chicken breasts and cook for 4–5 minutes on each side. Remove the chicken and set aside.

4   Add the remaining sliced onion and the remaining 1 sliced poblano pepper. Cook until tender, about 3–4 minutes. Reduce the heat to low and add the blender sauce. Bring to a simmer. Return the chicken to the skillet, cover, and allow to cook for 12–15 minutes.

5   Remove the skillet from the heat, remove the chicken, and allow to rest for 5–7 minutes before shredding with two forks.

6   Return the shredded chicken to the skillet. Lower the heat to low, stir, and simmer for 6 minutes until hot.

7   Serve on tostadas with toppings of choice.

Pork
Entrees

Tacos al Pastor..184

Carnitas..186

Chilorio..188

Tamales Verdes...189

Tamales Rojos...190

Pambazos de Papas con Chorizo...............................192

Tacos de Canasta..194

Ingredients

5 New Mexico peppers or guajillo peppers, cleaned and deseeded

1 ancho pepper, cleaned and deseeded

2oz (43g) achiote paste

¼ white onion

5 garlic cloves

3 whole cloves

1¼ tsp light brown sugar

1¼ tsp dried thyme

1¼ tsp dried oregano leaves

2½ tsp salt

1 tbsp white vinegar

2 tbsp vegetable oil

1 cup pineapple juice

juice of 1½ limes

3lb (1.4kg) pork shoulder, thinly sliced

18–24 tortillas

For serving

chopped fresh cilantro

diced pineapple

chopped white onion

salsa of choice

Tacos al Pastor

Shepherd-Style Tacos

◆ **Makes** 4–6 servings   ◆ **Ready in** 4–5 hours

Al pastor is a traditional Mexican dish that's made with grilled marinated meat and often served in tacos topped with cilantro, onions, and, let's not forget, grilled pineapple. The smoky and tangy flavors of this dish will keep you coming back for more. If you're not a fan of the pork used in this recipe, you can substitute chicken.

1   In a medium saucepan over medium-high heat, combine the New Mexico peppers and ancho pepper. Cover with water and allow to come to a boil. Once boiling, turn the heat off and drain the water. Allow to cool for about 15 minutes.

2   In a blender, combine the peppers, achiote paste, onion, garlic cloves, whole cloves, brown sugar, thyme, oregano, salt, vinegar, oil, pineapple juice, and lime juice. Blend on high until a marinade paste forms.

3   To a medium bowl, add the pork shoulder and completely coat with the marinade paste. Refrigerate for at least 4 hours.

4   Remove the pork from the fridge and let it come to room temperature, about 1 hour.

5   In a medium skillet over medium-high heat, cook the pork for 3–4 minutes on each side. Remove the skillet from the heat, cover with aluminum foil, and allow the pork to rest for 5 minutes.

6   Cut the meat into smaller strips and serve on a warm tortilla with your choice of taco toppings. I like to top mine with chopped cilantro, pineapple, onions, and salsa.

Ingredients

1lb (454g) lard

5 tsp salt or to taste

1 tbsp freshly ground black pepper or to taste

5 whole cloves

½ tsp ground cumin

4lb (1.8kg) pork shoulder, cut into large chunks

½ cup of water

1 cup evaporated milk

12oz (340g) Mexican Coca-Cola

juice of 1 orange, plus the peel

½ white onion

5 garlic cloves

4 bay leaves

2 sprigs of fresh thyme

2 sprigs of fresh rosemary

2 sprigs of fresh oregano

Carnitas

Slow-Cooked Pulled Pork

◆ **Makes** 6–8 servings

◆ **Ready in** 3 hours

Carnitas is a version of Mexican pulled pork that's slow-cooked in lard. In Mexico, this is done outside in a big cazo pot, but now it's easy to make in the comfort of your home. It's great in tacos, burritos, tortas, quesadillas, bowls, or gorditas—each bite is so flavorful. It might seem like an odd combination at first, but trust the process!

1   In a deep Dutch oven or skillet over medium-high heat, melt the lard. Once the lard has liquified, add the salt, pepper, cloves, and cumin. Mix well. Once the lard is hot, add the pork (in batches if needed) and cook for 4 minutes on each side.

2   Once the pork has browned, reduce the heat to medium-low. Add the water, evaporated milk, Mexican Coca-Cola, orange juice, orange peel, onion, garlic cloves, bay leaves, thyme, rosemary, and oregano. Allow to cook for 2 hours, or until the pork is tender and golden brown, stirring occasionally.

3   Remove the pork from the lard and let rest for 5–10 minutes. Discard the lard.

4   Chop the pork and serve as desired.

Chilorio

Chili-Braised Pork

✦ **Makes** 8–10 servings   ✦ **Ready in** 3 hours

This versatile recipe can be served for breakfast, lunch, or dinner—or at any family gathering. Think chorizo, but shred it! I love serving chilorio in tacos or with a side of rice and beans. You can also serve it on tostadas or really any way you see fit!

Ingredients

3–4lb (1.4–1.8kg) boneless pork shoulder, cut into chunks
1 tbsp salt
2 tsp freshly ground black pepper
4 chile de árbol peppers
4 pasilla peppers
4 guajillo peppers
½ white onion
10 whole allspice
½ tsp cumin seeds
1 tsp chicken bouillon
1 tsp dried Mexican oregano
5 garlic cloves
3 whole cloves
3 bay leaves, divided
1 tsp whole peppercorns
3 tbsp apple cider vinegar
1½ cups freshly squeezed orange juice
1 tbsp lard

For serving

tortillas
Mexican rice
refried beans
tostadas

1   In a large bowl, combine the pork shoulder, salt, and black pepper. Massage the seasonings into the meat and set aside.

2   In a small saucepan over high heat, combine the chile de árbol, pasilla and guajillo peppers, and onion. Cover with water and bring to a boil.

3   Once boiling, transfer everything to a blender. Add the whole allspice, whole cumin, chicken bouillon, Mexican oregano, garlic cloves, whole cloves, 1 bay leaf, whole peppercorns, apple cider vinegar, and orange juice. Blend on high until smooth. Set aside.

4   Preheat the oven to 325°F (160°C).

5   In a large, oven-safe pot or Dutch oven over high heat, melt the lard. Once the lard has melted, add the pork and sear the pork on all sides for 2–3 minutes, cooking in batches if needed. Once seared, cover the pork with the sauce from the blender. Add the remaining 2 bay leaves.

6   Cover with a lid and cook in the oven for 2½ hours or until the pork is fork-tender.

7   Remove the pot from the oven and discard the bay leaves. Shred the pork and serve as desired.

Tamales Verdes

Green Pork Tamales

✦ **Makes** 40 tamales   ✦ **Ready in** 5 hours

These are the most authentic green chili pork tamales if you ask me! If you don't own a pressure cooker, no worries. You can follow the steps as I did for the **Tamales Rojos** (page 190). These tamales are seriously super easy to make and perfect to surprise your family with during the holidays!

1   In a pressure cooker, combine the pork, head of garlic, 1 onion half, bay leaves, and 2 tablespoons of salt. Cover the pork to the max line with water (about 2½ quarts [2.4L]), close, set to sealing using the meat/stew setting, and cook for 90 minutes.

2   Allow the meat to sit for 20 minutes before shredding. Strain the broth. Set aside the meat and broth.

3   In a large saucepan over medium-high heat, combine the tomatillos and serrano peppers. Bring to a boil.

4   Transfer the tomatillos and serrano peppers to a blender. Add the garlic cloves, whole cloves, hatch peppers, cilantro, chicken bouillon, peppercorns, oregano, cumin seeds, 1 teaspoon salt, and the remaining onion half. Blend on high until smooth. Add ¾ cup of broth to the blender and blend again. Reserve 1 cup of the salsa.

5   In a medium frying pan over medium heat, heat the vegetable oil. Once hot, add the remaining sauce from the blender. Reduce the heat to medium-low and let simmer for 5 minutes.

6   Add the shredded pork and let simmer again. Set aside. Prepare the masa according to the recipe on page 81. Spread the masa in the center of each corn husk. Add 2 tablespoons of pork filling to each husk. Grab one end of each corn husk and fold it over the filling. Grab the other end and fold over to overlap it. Grab the tail of the corn husk and fold up.

7   Prep the steamer pot by adding water to the bottom of the pot and place 2 empty corn husks over the divider to block any water from getting to the tamales. Set on the stove over low heat.

8   Place the tamales in the steamer pot. Either stand them all up or stack them in a pyramid. Cover them with 4–5 empty corn husks and a kitchen towel. Cover with a sealed lid to trap the steam inside. Increase the heat to medium and let steam for 2 hours.

9   Remove the tamales from the steamer pot so the masa can set. Let sit for 10–15 minutes.

10 Serve with drizzled crema Mexicana and the reserved salsa.

Ingredients

7lb (3.2kg) pork shoulder, cut into chunks
1 head of garlic
1 white onion, halved, divided
4 bay leaves
3 tbsp plus 1 tsp salt, divided
15 tomatillos
2–5 serrano peppers
4 garlic cloves
3 whole cloves
6 green hatch peppers, roasted and peeled
½ bunch of fresh cilantro
2 tbsp chicken bouillon
1 tsp whole peppercorns
1 tsp dried oregano leaves
1 tsp cumin seeds
1 tbsp vegetable oil
1 batch of **Masa para Tamales** (page 81)
1lb (454g) corn husks, soaked

For serving
crema Mexicana
salsa (reserved)

Tip

You can substitute the pork shoulder with beef or chicken if you prefer. Just keep in mind that the cook time for chicken will be much shorter.

Ingredients

2 tbsp vegetable oil, for frying

1 batch **Masa para Tamales** (page 81)

1lb (454g) corn husks, soaked

For the broth

4 quarts (3.8L) water

1 white onion

1 head of garlic

4 bay leaves

2 tbsp plus 1 tsp salt, divided, plus more to taste

3 tbsp chicken bouillon, divided

5–6 lbs (2.3–2.7kg) pork shoulder, cut into large chunks

2 tsp whole peppercorns

2 tsp whole allspice

5 whole cloves

For the sauce

20 New Mexico peppers, cleaned and deveined

3 ancho peppers, cleaned and deveined

10 chile de árbol peppers (optional)

12 tomatillos, peeled and cleaned

7 garlic cloves

1½ tsp whole cumin seeds

Tip

Feel free to substitute beef chuck roast for the pork shoulder for a tasty variation of this recipe.

Tamales Rojos

Chili Colorado Tamales with Special Sauce

✦ **Makes** 35–40 tamales   ✦ **Ready in** 6 hours

This is my great-grandma's recipe and it's an honor to be able to share it with you and the world! When I first shared this recipe, everyone said I was doing it wrong, not knowing this has been a recipe passed down from generation to generation in my family. My great-grandma used to make them like this before passing it down to my grandma, who then passed it down to my mother, and so on. Please enjoy this deliciously unique recipe that means so much to me!

1   In a large pot over high heat, bring the water to a boil. Add the onion, head of garlic, bay leaves, 2 tablespoons of salt, 2 tablespoons of chicken bouillon, and pork. Return to a boil and strain any film that forms on the surface of the water.

2   Reduce the heat to medium and add the whole peppercorns, whole allspice, and whole cloves. Cover and allow to cook for 2 hours or until the pork is tender.

3   Remove the pork from the broth, shred, and set aside. Strain and reserve 4 cups of broth. Discard the rest.

4   In a medium saucepan over medium heat, combine the New Mexico peppers, ancho peppers, and tomatillos. Cover with water and bring to a boil.

5   Transfer the mixture to a blender. Add the reserved broth, garlic cloves, cumin seeds, the remaining 1 teaspoon of salt, and the remaining 1 tablespoon of chicken bouillon. Blend on high until smooth. Reserve 1 cup of sauce and set aside.

6   In a large skillet over medium-high heat, heat the vegetable oil. Once hot, add the meat and fry for 3 minutes. Add the sauce from the blender, straining if needed, reduce the heat to low, and simmer for 5 minutes. Taste for salt and adjust as needed. Set aside and let cool.

7   Prepare the masa according to the recipe on page 81. Be sure to use the reserved broth and the reserved chili pepper sauce.

8   Spread the masa in the center of each corn husk. Add 2 tablespoons of the pork filling to each husk. Grab one end of each corn husk and fold it over the filling. Grab the other end and fold over to overlap it. Grab the tail of the corn husk and fold up.

9   Prep the large steamer pot by adding water to the bottom of the pot and place 2 empty corn husks over the divider to block any water from getting to the tamales. Set on the stove over low heat.

10   Place the tamales in the steamer pot. Either stand them all up or stack them in a pyramid. Cover them with 4–5 empty corn husks and a kitchen towel. Cover with a sealed lid to trap the steam inside. Increase the heat to medium and let steam for 2 hours.

11   Remove the tamales from the steamer pot so the masa can set. Let sit for 10–15 minutes before serving.

Ingredients

4 medium russet potatoes, peeled and diced

salt, to taste

½ cup plus 2 tbsp vegetable oil, divided

1 white onion, chopped

3 Roma tomatoes, chopped

2 jalapeño peppers or serrano peppers, chopped

1lb (454g) chorizo

8 **Pan Bolillo rolls** (page 76)

For the sauce

10–15 guajillo peppers, cleaned and deseeded

½ white onion

2 garlic cloves

½ tsp dried oregano

¼ tsp ground cumin

¼ tsp freshly ground black pepper

salt, to taste

1 cup water

For serving

refried beans

shredded iceberg lettuce

crema Mexicana

Salsa Verde (page 98)

queso fresco

Pambazos de Papas con Chorizo

Chorizo and Potato Sandwich

✦ **Makes** 8 sandwiches   ✦ **Ready in** 30 minutes

Taking a bite of this delicious pambazo will transport your taste buds to the streets of Mexico. Bread dipped in guajillo sauce, fried, and stuffed with chorizo, potatoes, and other delectable fillings—what's not to love? So simple yet so delicious.

1   To make the sauce, to a small pot over high heat, add the guajillo peppers. Cover with water and bring to a boil.

2   Once boiling, transfer the peppers to a blender. Add the onion, garlic cloves, oregano, cumin, black pepper, salt to taste, and water. Blend on high until smooth.

3   Transfer the sauce to a small saucepan over medium-high heat, straining it if needed. Allow to simmer for 5 minutes. Taste for salt and adjust as needed. Remove the saucepan from the heat and set aside.

4   In a medium pot over medium heat, add the diced potatoes. Cover with water and bring to a boil. Season with salt to taste and cook for 5 minutes. Remove the pot from the heat and set aside.

5   In a large saucepan over medium-high heat, heat 2 tablespoons of vegetable oil. Once hot, add the onion, tomatoes, and jalapeño or serrano peppers. Sauté until tender. Once tender, add the chorizo, break it down, and cook for 5 minutes.

6   Use a strainer to strain the potatoes and add them to the saucepan. Cook until tender, about 5–6 minutes. Remove the saucepan from the heat and set aside.

7   On a griddle over medium heat, heat 1 tablespoon of vegetable oil. Once the oil is hot, split the rolls in half and dip the outsides of the halves into the sauce. Place the halves on the griddle, press down to flatten them, and fry for 2 minutes on each side. Remove the rolls from the griddle. Repeat for each sandwich, starting with adding another tablespoon of oil.

8   To make the sandwiches, add the chorizo con papa filling and other filling options of choice between the halves of the rolls. Repeat steps 7 and 8 for each sandwich.

Tacos de Canasta

Basket Tacos

Ingredients

4 medium russet potatoes, peeled and chopped

3 cups vegetable oil

1 white onion, sliced into thin strips, divided

1lb (454g) chorizo of your choice

salt, to taste

freshly ground black pepper, to taste

24 corn tortillas

For serving

Salsa Verde (page 98)

pickled jalapeños

pickled carrots

✦ **Makes** 24 tacos   ✦ **Ready in** 1 hour

These are the most popular tacos in Mexico City. Typically, these are stuffed with papas y chorizo (potatoes and sausage), beans, and cheese, but the most popular ones are made with chicharrón prensado (pressed pork skin). These tacos are prepared like regular tacos but are then placed in a basket, layered with a kitchen towel, plastic bag, and layers of butcher paper, and then covered in boiling oil. The end result is simply too delicious for words.

1   Place a long kitchen towel inside a Dutch oven, ensuring the towel lines the entire interior. Place a slow cooker liner or oven bag over the towel. Place about 2 large pieces of butcher paper or freezer paper over the towel.

2   In a medium saucepan over medium heat, add the potatoes, cover with water, and cook for 30–45 minutes. Drain.

3   In a separate medium saucepan over medium heat, combine the vegetable oil, ¼ of the onion, and chorizo. Cook for 5–7 minutes, breaking down the chorizo as it cooks. Add the cooked potatoes and season with salt and pepper to taste. Break down the potatoes until they're mashed with some chunks remaining, mix everything together, and cook for 2 more minutes. Reduce the heat to the lowest setting.

4   Heat the tortillas in a griddle/skillet for about 15 seconds on each side. Add 2 tablespoons of the chorizo and potato filling to each tortilla. Fold and begin to layer the tacos in the Dutch oven.

5   Once all the tacos have been placed, add the rest of the onion, then carefully pour the boiling oil over the tacos. Cover with more butcher paper, a plastic bag, another kitchen towel, and the lid. Allow to steep for 5–10 minutes.

6   Serve with **Salsa Verde** (page 98), pickled jalapeños, and pickled carrots. Discard the oil in the Dutch oven when finished.

Seafood, Veggie & Egg Entrees

Camarónes a la Diabla 198

Tacos de Camarón 200

Tacos Gobernador 202

Tacos de Pescado 204

Tamales de Rajas con Queso 205

Chile Rellenos 206

Enchiladas Rojas 208

Enfrijoladas 210

Migas a la Mexicana 212

Ingredients

4 Roma tomatoes

4 chile de árbol peppers

4 guajillo peppers

1 white onion, divided

2–4 chipotle peppers in adobo
  sauce

1 garlic clove

2 tbsp salted butter

salt, to taste

freshly ground black pepper,
  to taste

2lb (907g) medium raw
  shrimp, peeled and deveined

For serving

cooked white rice

Camarónes a la Diabla

Deviled Shrimp

✦ **Makes** 4–6 servings   ✦ **Ready in** 30 minutes

This has to be my favorite shrimp recipe! The name says it all. This super easy recipe has the tastiest spicy chipotle sauce. While I love it, if you're not a fan of this spice level, you can adjust this recipe by eliminating the chile de árbol peppers and only adding one chipotle pepper. For spice lovers like me, try replacing the guajillo peppers with New Mexico peppers.

1   In a medium saucepan over medium heat, combine the tomatoes, chile de árbol peppers, and guajillo peppers. Cover with water and bring to a boil. Once boiling, turn off the heat and allow the tomatoes and peppers to cool. Discard the water.

2   In a blender, combine the cooled tomatoes and peppers, ¼ of the onion, chipotle peppers in adobo sauce, and garlic. Blend on high to purée and set aside.

3   In a large skillet over medium heat, melt the butter. Once the butter has melted, add the rest of the onion and sauté until translucent. Add the shrimp, season with salt and pepper to taste, and cook for 2–3 minutes.

4   Stir in the sauce from the blender and simmer on low for 3–5 minutes.

5   Serve over your preferred amount of white rice.

Ingredients

2lb (907g) colossal raw shrimp, cleaned, peeled, and deveined
salt, to taste
freshly ground black pepper, to taste
2 cups vegetable oil
10–12 tortillas

For the spicy salsa

1 handful of tepin peppers (about 7g)
juice of ½ a lemon
½ cup mayo
½ cup sour cream

For the batter

2 cups all-purpose flour
1½ tsp baking powder
1½ tsp garlic salt
1½ tsp California chili powder
1½ tsp dried oregano
1½ tsp freshly ground black pepper
2 whole eggs
1 (12oz [340g]) can of beer of choice
1½ tsp mustard

For serving

shredded purple cabbage
Pico de Gallo (page 92)
pickled onions

Tacos de Camarón

Baja Shrimp Tacos

◆ **Makes** 6 servings   ◆ **Ready in** 45 minutes

Tacos are life! And these are the ultimate shrimp tacos. The combination of the battered shrimp, pico de gallo, cabbage, and salsa brings the flavor of these tacos together, making it possible for everyone to enjoy them.

1   To make the salsa, to a blender, add the tepin peppers and blend on high until fully crushed. Add the lemon juice, mayo, and sour cream. Blend on high until a smooth salsa forms. Set aside.

2   Place the shrimp in a large bowl and season to taste with the salt and black pepper. Set aside.

3   To make the batter, in a large bowl, whisk together the flour, baking powder, garlic salt, chili powder, oregano, and black pepper. Slowly whisk in the beer, then the eggs, and then the mustard. The batter should be well-hydrated.

4   Add half the shrimp to the batter bowl and mix until all are coated. Remove and set aside before repeating with the second half.

5   In a medium frying pan over medium heat, heat the vegetable oil until it reaches 350°F (177°C). Add the shrimp and fry for 2–3 minutes on each side or until the batter is golden brown. Remove any excess oil before serving.

6   Serve on a warm tortilla with a bed of spicy salsa and the desired amount of shrimp. Top with shredded purple cabbage, **Pico de Gallo** (page 92), pickled onions, and more spicy salsa. Feel free to get creative with your own desired toppings.

Tacos Gobernador

Cheesy Shrimp Tacos

Ingredients

2 tbsp salted butter

¼ white onion, finely chopped

1 serrano pepper or jalapeño pepper, diced

2 garlic cloves, minced

2 Roma tomatoes, diced

1 poblano pepper, roasted, peeled, and chopped into small cubes

1lb (454g) (26–30) large raw shrimp, peeled, cleaned, and deveined

1½ tbsp prepackaged roasted garlic and herbs seasoning

1 tsp freshly ground black pepper

2 tbsp chopped fresh cilantro

1 tbsp vegetable oil, for frying

10 corn tortillas

1lb (454g) grated queso Oaxaca or Monterey Jack cheese

For serving

Salsa Verde (page 98)

✦ **Makes** 10 tacos   ✦ **Ready in** 20 minutes

These tacos are out of this world! And the story behind them is even more interesting. These tasty tacos were created in a famous restaurant in Sinaloa back in the day to impress the governor. Essentially a grilled quesadilla stuffed with a hearty shrimp and poblano mixture, these tacos are perfect when you want something fast and delicious.

1   In a medium frying pan over medium heat, melt the butter. Once hot, add the onion and serrano, and sauté for 2 minutes. Add the garlic and cook for 1 minute more. Add the tomatoes and the poblano. Stir and cook for 2 minutes more.

2   Add the shrimp, garlic and herbs seasoning, black pepper, and cilantro. Stir and cook the shrimp for 2–3 minutes or until they begin to turn an opaque salmon color.

3   In a large skillet over medium heat, heat the vegetable oil. Once hot, place a tortilla in the skillet and allow it to blister. Flip the tortilla and cover with shredded cheese. Once the cheese has melted, add some of the vegetables to half the tortilla. Place 3 shrimp on top of the vegetables and close. Repeat until all the tacos have formed.

4   Serve with **Salsa Verde** (page 98) to taste.

Ingredients

4 cups vegetable oil

2lb (907g) Alaskan cod fillets, halved lengthwise and patted dry

12 flour tortillas

For the dry mixture

1 cup all-purpose flour

2 tbsp cornstarch

1 tsp salt

1 tsp freshly cracked black pepper

For the wet batter

⅔ cup all-purpose flour

20–22 saltine crackers, pulverized

¼ tsp baking powder

½ tsp salt

½ tsp freshly ground black pepper

½ tsp onion powder

1 tsp chili powder

1 tsp dried oregano

1 tsp garlic salt

1 whole egg

12oz (340g) beer or mineral water

For serving

shredded cabbage

salsa of choice

Tacos de Pescado

Beer-Battered Fish Tacos

✦ **Makes** 12 tacos   ✦ **Ready in** 30 minutes

Grab a cold beer to enjoy with these delicious fish tacos. This recipe honors my mom's preference of using saltine crackers to help the fish come out a bit crispier. I recommend Modelo if you're looking for a flavorful beer for the batter. If you're looking for a nonalcoholic option, mineral water will also work.

1   To make the dry mixture, in a medium baking dish, combine the dry mixture ingredients and mix well. Set aside.

2   To make the wet batter, in a separate medium baking dish, combine the flour, crackers, baking powder, salt, black pepper, onion powder, chili powder, oregano, and garlic salt. Mix well. Add the egg and beer. Mix well again.

3   In a large frying pan, heat the vegetable oil to 350°F (177°C).

4   Coat a cod fillet with the dry flour mixture and dip into the wet batter, ensuring to cover the fillet with batter. Immediately fry the fillets for 3–4 minutes or until golden brown.

5   Serve in a warm tortilla and top with shredded cabbage and your choice of salsa.

Tamales de Rajas con Queso

Poblano Rajas and Cheese Tamales

~~~~~~

◆ **Makes** 35–40 tamales ◆ **Ready in** 3 hours

~~~~~~

Tamales are a favorite in my family during fall and winter. I don't make them unless it's that time of year because they simply hit differently when the weather is colder! One of our favorite variations of tamales is one with rajas (pepper strips) and cheese. Let me tell you, these are a lot faster to make than any meat varieties. Perfect to try if you have never made tamales before, tamales de rajas con queso is certainly a crowd-pleaser!

Ingredients

2 large slicing tomatoes, roasted

4 Roma tomatoes, roasted

4–6 serrano peppers or jalapeño peppers, roasted

3 garlic cloves

1 tbsp chicken bouillon

¼ tsp ground cumin

1 tbsp vegetable oil

1 white onion, sliced

10 poblano peppers, roasted, peeled, and cut into bite-size strips

salt, to taste

1 batch of **Masa para Tamales** (page 81)

45 corn husks

30oz (850g) shredded queso Oaxaca or Monterey Jack cheese

For serving

crema Mexicana

salsa of choice

1   In a blender, combine the tomatoes, serrano peppers, garlic, chicken bouillon, and cumin. Blend on high until smooth.

2   In a large skillet, heat the vegetable oil. Once hot, add the onion and sauté for 3 minutes.

3   Add the poblano peppers and season with salt to taste. Cook for 2 minutes. Add the tomato sauce from the blender and simmer for 5 minutes more.

4   Prepare the masa according to the recipe on page **81**.

5   Spread the masa in the center of each corn husk. Add the shredded cheese and 2 tablespoons of the pepper mixture. Fold the long sides of the corn husk in and then fold the top over.

6   Prep the steamer pot by adding water to the bottom of the pot and place 2 empty corn husks over the divider to block any water from getting to the tamales. Set on the stove over low heat.

7   Place the tamales in the steamer pot. Either stand them all up or stack them in a pyramid. Cover them with 2 empty corn husks and a kitchen towel. Cover with a sealed lid, trapping the steam inside. Increase the heat to medium and let steam for 2 hours.

8   Remove the tamales from the steamer pot so the masa can set. Let sit for 10–15 minutes. Unwrap them and discard the empty corn husks.

9   Serve with drizzled crema Mexicana and salsa of your choice.

Ingredients

6 poblano peppers

6 cups plus 1 tbsp vegetable oil, divided

2lb (907g) shredded queso Oaxaca cheese

3 tbsp all-purpose flour, plus more for dusting

6 eggs, separated, room temperature

½ tsp salt

For the sauce

4 Roma tomatoes

5–10 chile de árbol peppers

1–3 serrano peppers or jalapeño peppers

¼ white onion

3 garlic cloves

½ tsp dried oregano

1 tsp chicken bouillon

salt, to taste

1 cup water

For the stuffing

1 tbsp vegetable oil

½ white onion, finely chopped

2 Roma tomatoes, finely chopped

1–2 serrano peppers or jalapeño peppers, finely chopped

For serving

Mexican rice

queso fresco

chopped cilantro

Chile Rellenos

Stuffed Poblano Peppers

◆ **Makes** 6 servings   ◆ **Ready in** 1 hour

This is a traditional Mexican dish. Preparing it can be a little time consuming, but let me tell you, it's worth every minute. The best chile rellenos are homemade and no restaurant will serve them better than this. The best way to enjoy this meal is as soon as they leave the oil bath, the cheese has melted, and the egg is nice and fluffy. Chiles rellenos can be a little intimidating, but after you get the egg batter to perfection, it will be just as easy as making a quesadilla.

1   On a small griddle over medium heat, char the poblano peppers. Once charred, place the peppers in a resealable plastic bag and allow to sweat for 15 minutes.

2   To make the sauce, in a small pot over medium-high heat, combine the tomatoes and all the peppers. Cover with water and bring to a boil. Remove the tomatoes and peppers and discard the boiling water.

3   In a blender, combine the tomatoes, peppers, onion, garlic, oregano, chicken bouillon, salt, and water. Blend on high until smooth.

4   In a medium saucepan over medium heat, heat 2 tablespoons of vegetable oil. Once hot, add the sauce from the blender and bring to a simmer. Taste for salt and add more as needed. Set aside.

5   Remove the poblanos from the bag and carefully remove the skin from each. Cut a small slit from the top of each pepper to about 1 inch from the end. Be careful not to cut all the way down to preserve the filling. Remove the seeds carefully and set aside.

6   To make the stuffing, in a small saucepan on medium heat, heat 1 tablespoon of vegetable oil. Once hot, add the chopped onion, chopped tomatoes, and chopped serrano peppers. Sauté for 3 minutes. Stir in the queso Oaxaca.

7   Stuff the cheese mixture into each poblano, making sure each pepper is fully stuffed. Dust the peppers with a little flour and set aside.

8   In a large saucepan over medium-low heat, heat 6 cups of vegetable oil.

9   In a large glass bowl, add the egg whites, setting the yolks aside. Use a hand or stand mixer to beat the egg whites on medium speed until stiff peaks form, about 3–5 minutes.

10   Add the egg yolks, 3 tablespoons of flour, and salt. Beat on low speed until well incorporated. The egg batter should be light, fluffy, and yellow.

11   Increase the oil heat to medium and ensure it's still hot.

12   Grab a poblano by the stem and dip the pepper in the egg batter. Be sure to fully coat the pepper. Gently transfer the poblano to the oil and fry on both sides until golden, about 2 minutes per side. Drain excess oil in paper towels and repeat until all the peppers have been fried.

13   Add a little sauce to each serving plate and place a chile relleno on top of each. Serve with a side of rice and garnish with queso fresco and cilantro.

Ingredients

8 New Mexico, California, or guajillo peppers, cleaned and deveined

2 pasilla peppers or ancho peppers, cleaned and deveined

4 chile de árbol peppers

¾ white onion (¼ whole and ½ finely chopped)

2 garlic cloves

¼ tsp whole cumin

½ tsp dried oregano

½ tsp whole peppercorns

3 cups water

1 tbsp plus ½ cup vegetable oil, divided

salt, to taste

16oz (454g) queso fresco, crumbled

25–30 corn tortillas

For serving

Arroz Rojo (page 66)

refried beans

crema Mexicana

queso fresco

chopped purple or white onion

chopped Roma tomato

shredded iceberg lettuce

Enchiladas Rojas

Red Enchiladas

✦ **Makes** 25–30 enchiladas   ✦ **Ready in** 1 hour

Enchiladas rojas is one of my favorite dishes of them all! My grandma made them best and this recipe is very special to me because it was one of the last she taught me. Like most of the recipes in this book, these enchiladas are simple, easy, and so delicious! Who would have thought a lightly fried tortilla dipped in a guajillo sauce and stuffed with cheese and onion could be as enjoyable as it is?

1   In a medium saucepan over medium-high heat, add all the peppers and cover with water. Bring to a boil. Discard the water.

2   In a blender, combine the peppers, ¼ white onion, garlic, cumin, oregano, peppercorns, and water. Blend on high until smooth.

3   In a medium frying pan over medium-low heat, heat 1 tablespoon of vegetable oil. Once hot, add the sauce from the blender, straining as needed. Add the salt and bring the sauce to a simmer. Reduce the heat to low and simmer for 10 minutes more. Set aside.

4   In a small bowl, combine the chopped onion and queso fresco. Set aside.

5   In a small frying pan over medium heat, heat the remaining ½ cup of vegetable oil. Once hot, carefully add a tortilla and lightly fry until it blisters, about 10 seconds. Remove the tortilla and place it between paper towels, allowing it to drain the excess oil. Repeat until all the tortillas have been fried.

6   Dip each fried tortilla in the pepper sauce, add about 2 tablespoons of cheese mixture, and roll to form a flute. Repeat until all the tortillas have been rolled.

7   Serve with **Arroz Rojo** (page 66) and refried beans. Top with your favorite toppings, such as crema Mexicana, queso fresco, chopped onion, chopped tomato, shredded lettuce, or any remaining pepper sauce before serving.

Ingredients

1 cup uncooked pinto, Peruvian, or black beans, cleaned, or 3 cups precooked beans

¼ white onion

1 garlic clove

4 New Mexico peppers

2 morita peppers or chipotle peppers in adobo sauce

2 tsp salt

1 tsp freshly ground black pepper

½ tsp dried oregano

3 tbsp vegetable oil, divided

25 corn tortillas

2lb (907g) queso fresco, crumbled

½ red onion, chopped

For serving

crema Mexicana

crumbled queso fresco

Pico de Gallo (page 92)

avocado slices

Enfrijoladas

Bean Sauce Enchiladas

◆ **Makes** 25 enfrijoladas   ◆ **Ready in** 70 minutes

Very similar to enchiladas, this variation differs with a delicious, creamy bean sauce. Simple and easy, this recipe and its versatility have gotten me out of so many situations when I really didn't feel like cooking. If you have leftover beans, this recipe is done in less than 15 minutes! But don't worry if not—I'll show you how to make fresh beans with a pressure cooker.

1   In a pressure cooker, combine the beans, white onion, and garlic. Close the lid, set to sealing, and use the bean setting to cook for 45 minutes on high. Allow to sit for 20 minutes. Release any steam and open.

2   In a medium skillet over medium heat, combine the New Mexico peppers and morita peppers. (If you use chipotle peppers, include the adobo sauce.) Toast for 30 seconds or until they puff. Stir the peppers into the beans and let rest for 5 minutes.

3   In a blender, combine the beans, peppers, salt, black pepper, and oregano. Blend on high until smooth. (If using precooked beans, add the white onion and garlic to the blender here, along with the precooked beans and toasted peppers.)

4   In a large frying pan over medium heat, heat 1 tablespoon of vegetable oil. Once hot, add the bean and pepper sauce. Bring to a simmer. Taste and adjust for salt as needed. Continue simmering for 5 minutes more or until the sauce thickens.

5   On a griddle over medium heat, heat the remaining 2 tablespoons of vegetable oil. Add a tortilla and lightly fry on each side for about 10 seconds. Repeat until all the tortillas have been fried.

6   In a small bowl, combine the queso fresco and red onion.

7   Dip a fried tortilla in the bean sauce, stuff with 2 tablespoons of the cheese mixture, and roll to form a flute. Repeat with the remaining tortillas.

8   Add bean sauce to each serving plate and place three enfrijoladas on top. Cover with more bean sauce and top with crema Mexicana, queso fresco, **Pico de Gallo** (page 92), and avocado slices before serving.

Ingredients

3 tbsp vegetable oil

10 corn tortillas, cut into
1.5-inch (3.9 cm) squares

8oz (227g) chorizo

1 Roma tomato, diced

¼ white onion, diced

1 red bell pepper, diced

1 serrano pepper or jalapeño
pepper, diced

salt, to taste

freshly ground black pepper,
to taste

10–12 whole eggs, beaten

Mexican blend cheese of
choice

For serving

refried beans

Migas a la Mexicana

Mexican-Style Scrambled Eggs and Chips

✦ **Makes** 6–7 servings

✦ **Ready in** 20 minutes

Migas a la Mexicana is seriously everything you want in an egg dish. Growing up, my mom would make this for the family and we'd never get tired of it because she made it differently every time! In addition to this variation, my mom would sometimes add frijoles de la olla or switch it up by adding chorizo or ham.

1   In a large, deep skillet over medium-high heat, heat the vegetable oil. Once hot, add the tortilla squares and fry for 5–6 minutes until golden brown.

2   Remove excess oil from the pan, add the chorizo, and cook for 3 minutes. Add the tomato, onion, bell pepper, and serrano pepper. Cook for 5 minutes more. Once the bell peppers are tender, add the eggs and cook and scramble until they reach your desired consistency. Top with the cheese, cover with a lid, and cook until the cheese melts.

3   Serve with refried beans.

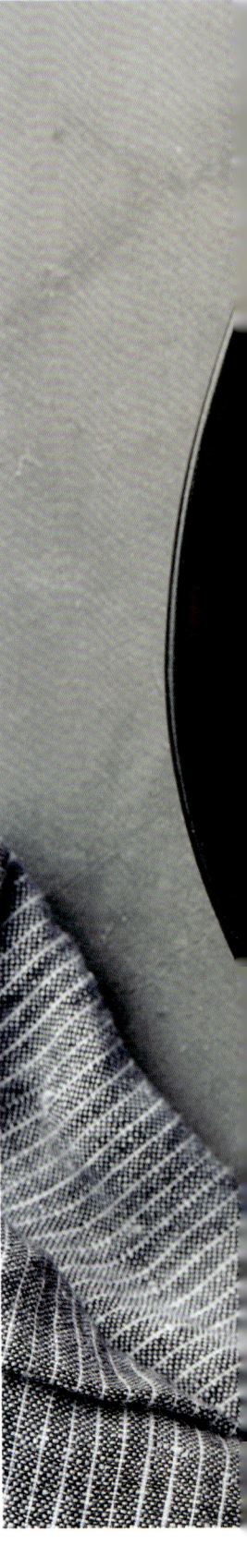

Desserts

Arroz con Leche 216

Bionicos 218

Fresas con Crema 220

Gelatina de Mosaico 222

Gelatina Fresas con Crema 224

Churros 225

Buñuelos 226

Choco Flan 228

Pastel Tres Leches 230

Arroz con Leche

Rice Pudding

◆ **Makes** 8 servings ◆ **Ready in** 50 minutes

Ingredients

6 cups water
¼ tsp salt
2 cinnamon sticks
½ cup granulated sugar
2 cups uncooked long-grain rice, rinsed and cleaned
6 cups whole milk
1 (12oz [340g]) can of evaporated milk
1 (14oz [397g]) can of sweetened condensed milk

For serving

ground cinnamon
fresh fruits
dry fruits

Arroz con leche is a traditional dessert that can be enjoyed at any time of the day. When its fragrant aroma fills the air, it ignites my spirit with childhood memories of eating this delicious treat for breakfast. A dish of delectably creamy arroz con leche enjoyed with a delicious **Café de la Olla** (page 44) is a perfect way to start your day. This recipe can be made as thick as pudding or as runny as you wish, and it can also be enjoyed hot or cold. This version is how my grandma used to make it for us, but if you want it to be thick, add only 3 cups of milk. Just keep in mind that as it sits, it thickens up!

1   In a large pot over medium-high heat, combine the water, salt, and cinnamon sticks. Bring to a boil.

2   Once the water comes to a boil, add the rice and sugar, and cook for 20 minutes.

3   Once the water has reduced, lower the heat to medium-low and add the whole milk, evaporated milk, and sweetened condensed milk. Mix and allow to cook for 25 minutes more or until the rice is tender, stirring often to prevent the rice from sticking to the bottom of the pot and burning.

4   Garnish with your choice of toppings. (Cinnamon is my favorite.) Serve hot.

Ingredients

10 cups chopped fresh fruit of choice (such as apples, pineapples, mangoes, melons, bananas, kiwis, papayas, and strawberries)

½ cup vanilla yogurt

½ cup Mexican table cream

7oz (198g) sweetened condensed milk

1 tsp Mexican vanilla blend

For serving

granola

coconut flakes

chopped pecans

Bionicos

Fruit and Cream Salad

〰〰〰〰〰〰〰〰〰〰〰〰〰

- ◆ **Makes** 8 servings
- ◆ **Ready in** 5 minutes

〰〰〰〰〰〰〰〰〰〰〰〰〰

Bionicos are perfect for breakfast, dessert, or snacks. They're easy to make and are something the whole family will enjoy. You can choose your favorite fruits to add to this dessert to make it festive for the holidays or special occasions. I personally love a tropical combination of kiwis, mangoes, bananas, pineapples, and papayas, sprinkled with sweetened coconut flakes and topped with granola. I swear I can eat this all day.

1   Add the fruit to a large bowl and set aside.

2   In a medium bowl, combine the yogurt, table cream, condensed milk, and vanilla blend. Mix well.

3   To a large serving dish, add most of the yogurt mixture to the bottom of the dish. Add the chopped fruit, and drizzle the remaining yogurt mixture over the top. Add your choice of toppings before serving. (Pecans are my favorite.)

Ingredients

1 cup crema Mexicana

1 (12oz [340g]) can of
evaporated milk

1 (14oz [397g]) can of
sweetened condensed milk

2 tbsp Mexican vanilla blend

1lb (454g) fresh strawberries,
hulled and thinly sliced

For serving

granola

Fresas con Crema

Strawberries and Cream

✦ **Ready in** 65 minutes   ✦ **Makes** 6–8 servings

This is one of the desserts my kids crave all summer long. The best part is I always have these ingredients on hand. You really can't go wrong with fresh strawberries mixed with a smooth, sweetened cream and topped with granola. It's seriously so simple yet so delicious—the only hard part about this recipe is the wait time! Allowing the cream to chill allows it to thicken up a bit, but to be honest, we rarely wait. I'll often make creamy sauce and refrigerate it while I wash, clean, and cut my strawberries, which gives it a few minutes to chill.

1   In a large bowl, combine the crema Mexicana, evaporated milk, condensed milk, and vanilla blend. Mix for a couple minutes or until fully combined.

2   Stir in the strawberries and refrigerate for at least 1 hour or until completely chilled.

3   Top with granola before serving.

Ingredients

4 cups hot water

2 (6oz [170g]) boxes of gelatin powder of choice, two different flavors

4 cups ice-cold water

½ cup room temperature water

1oz (28g) unflavored gelatin powder

1 (12oz [340g]) can of evaporated milk

1 cup media crema (table cream)

1 (14oz [397]) can of sweetened condensed milk

2 tbsp Mexican vanilla blend

Gelatina de Mosaico

Mosaic Gelatin

~~~~~~

◆ **Makes** 8 servings   ◆ **Ready in** 8 hours (or overnight)

~~~~~~

This wonderful dessert is made with different colors of flavored gelatin mixed with unflavored gelatin and uses the famous three kinds of milk: condensed, evaporated, and media crema. It's super easy and so delicious. It's the perfect dessert to share at your family gatherings, parties, or any other occasion.

1   In a medium saucepan, bring the hot water to a boil, then divide the water (2 cups each) into two separate containers. Whisk a gelatin packet into each container until fully dissolved. Once the gelatin has dissolved, whisk 2 cups of ice-cold water into each container until fully mixed.

2   Pour each prepared gelatin into an 8 x 8-inch (20 x 20 cm) pan and refrigerate until the gelatin has fully set. Once set, cut into small squares and set aside.

3   In a small mixing bowl, whisk together the room temperature water and unflavored gelatin. Once thickened, microwave the mixture for 20 seconds or until liquefied.

4   In a blender, combine the unflavored gelatin mixture, evaporated milk, media crema, sweetened condensed milk, and vanilla. Blend on medium speed for 20 seconds or until fully mixed. Set aside.

5   Spray a 12-cup Bundt pan with nonstick cooking spray and remove any excess with a paper towel. Layer the pan with the milk mixture and the gelatin squares until full. Refrigerate for a minimum of 4 hours or until the mixture is firm and set. Serve chilled.

Ingredients

4 cups hot water, divided

6oz (170g) strawberry gelatin powder

6oz (170g) lime gelatin powder

4 cups ice-cold water, divided

1 (14oz [397g]) can of sweetened condensed milk

1 cup vanilla yogurt

1 cup heavy whipping cream

1 cup sour cream

1 (12oz [340g]) can of evaporated milk

1 tbsp Mexican vanilla blend

2–3lb (907g–1.4kg) strawberries, hulled and sliced

For serving

granola

sweetened coconut flakes

chopped almonds

chopped pecans

Gelatina Fresas con Crema

Strawberries and Cream Gelatin

✦ **Makes** 8 servings   ✦ **Ready in** 5 hours

This easy and delicious dessert is sweet, creamy, and refreshing. You really can't go wrong with fresh strawberries and gelatin cubes mixed with a smooth, sweetened cream. The best part is you can change the flavor and color of this delicious dessert according to the holiday or special occasion you're celebrating, so get creative! This recipe calls for strawberry and lime gelatin, but feel free to use the flavors you love most.

1   In a medium bowl, whisk together 2 cups of hot water and the strawberry gelatin powder. Stir in 2 cups of the ice-cold water. Repeat with the remaining hot water, lime gelatin powder, and the remaining cold water.

2   Spray two 9- x 13-inch (23 x 33 cm) baking dishes with nonstick cooking spray and remove any excess with a paper towel. Pour each gelatin mix into separate dishes. Refrigerate for at least 4 hours or overnight.

3   In a blender, combine the condensed milk, yogurt, whipping cream, sour cream, evaporated milk, and vanilla blend. Blend on high until smooth. Transfer the mixture to a large bowl and refrigerate for at least 30 minutes.

4   Cut the chilled gelatins into squares. In a large bowl, combine all the gelatin squares, cream mixture, and strawberries. Mix until combined and refrigerate for 30 minutes more. Serve with your toppings of choice.

Churros

+ **Makes** 16 churros   + **Ready in** 50 minutes

Making churros is super easy and delicious, which means it's the perfect dessert for your family or for larger gatherings. When making churros, you can get as creative as you want—from stuffing the churros with your favorite fillings or syrups to serving them as an ice cream sundae or simply enjoying them plain. The best part is you don't have to wait for the fair to enjoy a delicious churro and you can make them as big as you want.

1   In a medium saucepan over medium heat, combine the butter, water, vanilla extract, 1 tablespoon of sugar, and salt. Once the butter has melted, reduce the heat to low and add the flour. Stir until a dough has formed. Turn off the heat and allow the dough to cool to room temperature.

2   Transfer the dough to the bowl of a stand mixer. Add the eggs one at a time until fully incorporated. Add the dough to a piping bag fitted with a large star attachment.

3   In a medium frying pan over medium heat, add the oil. Once hot, pipe the churro mixture in 8-inch-long (20 cm) lines, cutting them with kitchen scissors, and allow to cook for 4–7 minutes or until golden brown. Transfer the churros to a wire rack placed on a baking sheet.

4   In a small bowl, combine the cinnamon and the remaining ½ cup of sugar. Dip the churros into this mixture once the oil has drained from them but while still hot. Serve warm.

Ingredients

1 stick (8 tbsp) unsalted butter
1 cup water or (½ cup whole milk and ½ cup water)
½ tsp pure vanilla extract
1 tbsp plus ½ cup granulated sugar
¼ tsp salt
1½ cups all-purpose flour
3 large eggs
5 cups canola oil or frying oil of choice
1–2 tbsp ground cinnamon

Ingredients

3½ cups all-purpose flour

1½ tsp baking powder

¾ tsp salt

½ cup all-vegetable shortening at room temperature

1 cup granulated sugar, divided

1 egg at room temperature

2 tbsp Mexican vanilla blend

8.5oz (250ml) Mexican Fanta soda, water, or milk (see Note)

8 cups vegetable oil

1 tbsp ground cinnamon

Buñuelos

Mexican Fritters

♦ **Makes** 12–16 buñuelos   ♦ **Ready in** 4 hours

It's not the holidays without buñuelos—crispy fritters that are a traditional Mexican dessert you can enjoy year-round. Served with hot chocolate, **Atole de Galletas** (page 50), coffee, or even piloncillo syrup or ice cream, this is a versatile dessert that can be presented in many ways. Now let me tell you, making buñuelos is as special as making tamales; it's a long process, but the time spent as a family is unforgettable.

1   In a large bowl, combine the flour, baking powder, salt, shortening, and 1½ teaspoons sugar, and mix until combined. The shortening should be crumbled in with the flour.

2   Form a hole in the center of your flour mixture and add the egg and vanilla blend. Mix everything together until the mixture resembles coarse sand.

3   Slowly add the soda until the dough is well hydrated. Knead for about 5 minutes or until the dough is soft and doesn't stick to your hands. Cover the dough and allow to rest for 20 minutes.

4   Divide the dough into 28 golf ball–sized balls and cover with plastic wrap and a kitchen towel.

5   After 25 minutes, uncover the balls and use a rolling pin to roll them into thin, almost transparent circles. Allow them to rest uncovered for a few hours or until they're fully dried out on both sides.

6   Once the buñuelos are dried out, use a fork to poke several holes into each fritter to prevent large bubbles.

7   To a large frying pan over medium heat, add the oil. Once the oil is hot, fry for 1 minute on each side or until the buñuelos are golden and crispy.

8   In a small bowl, combine the remaining sugar and cinnamon. Remove the buñuelos from the pan and sprinkle them with the cinnamon sugar while still hot. Serve warm.

Note

Mexican orange soda contains cane sugar, which is sweeter and helps with the dough.

Choco Flan

Impossible Flan Cake

Ingredients

4oz (113g) cream cheese, softened

1 (14oz [397]) can of sweetened condensed milk

pinch of salt

4 large eggs at room temperature

1 (12oz [340g]) can of evaporated milk

1 tbsp pure vanilla extract

¾–1 cup cajeta (caramel)

1 box of chocolate cake mix or cake mix of choice and all its needed ingredients

For serving

caramel sauce

chopped nuts

chopped fresh fruit

✦ **Makes** 8–10 servings ✦ **Ready in** 4 hours 10 minutes

This is a must-have dessert for every special occasion and family gathering. And you can make it in so many ways—from adding cajeta (caramel sauce) to coconut milk to Nutella. I do the method differently than most because the presentation is everything to me. When you cut into this cake, the separation between the flan and cake must be clean. Once you make the cake, you can get creative and top it with more caramel, nuts, fresh fruit, and so on.

1   Preheat oven to 350°F (180°C). Spray a 9-cup Bundt pan with nonstick cooking spray and remove any excess with a paper towel. Place the pan in a large roasting pan filled halfway with water and set aside.

2   In a large bowl, combine the cream cheese, condensed milk, and salt, and mix until no lumps remain. Whisk in the eggs until fully combined. Add the evaporated milk and vanilla, and mix again.

3   Pour the cajeta into the Bundt pan, scooping out any that clings to the bowl, followed by the flan mixture. Place in the oven to bake for 45 minutes.

4   If using a cake mix, follow the instructions on the package.

5   Remove the flan from oven, slowly pour the cake mix on top of the flan, and cover with aluminum foil sprayed with nonstick cooking spray. Bake for 45 minutes more.

6   After 45 minutes, make sure the cake is fully baked by inserting a toothpick in the center. If it comes out clean, the cake is done. Remove the pan from the water bath and allow it to cool down (usually 2 hours).

7   Place a flat plate on the top of the Bundt pan and flip it over slowly. Lift the pan to separate the flan from the pan. Serve chilled.

Ingredients

1 box of vanilla cake mix and all its ingredients

2 tbsp Mexican vanilla blend, divided

1 cup media crema (table cream)

1 (14oz [397]) can of sweetened condensed milk

1 (12oz [340g]) can of evaporated milk

For serving

whipped topping

ground cinnamon

3 cups fruit of choice

Pastel Tres Leches

Three Milk Cake

✦ **Makes** 12 servings   ✦ **Ready in** 8 hours

This cake is a party staple—there's no celebration without it. This recipe is super easy, using store-bought cake mix—but who doesn't like a little shortcut when it gets you amazing results? You can make your own whipped topping or use store-bought to make it even easier! You can also get creative and switch the flavor profile by enhancing the flavor of the three milks or changing the cake mix flavor. Regardless, this is a dessert you must try—it's honestly the best!

1   Preheat the oven to 350°F (180°C).

2   Using a baking dish, follow the instructions on the cake box and use all its required ingredients, plus 1 tablespoon Mexican vanilla blend. Bake and allow to cool to room temperature before continuing.

3   In a large bowl, combine the media crema, sweetened condensed milk, evaporated milk, and remaining tablespoon of Mexican vanilla blend. Mix until well combined and set aside.

4   Use a fork to poke holes throughout the cake to allow the milk to seep through. Slowly pour the milk mixture onto the cake and allow it to seep to the bottom of the pan. Continue this process until you've reached your desired wetness of the cake or until all the milk mixture is gone.

5   Cover with aluminum foil and refrigerate for at least 6 hours or overnight.

6   Top the cake with whipped topping, cinnamon, and your choice of fruit before serving. (Strawberries are my favorite.)

Index

A

Agua Fresca de Hibisco con Fresas (Strawberry Hibiscus Water), 36

Agua Fresca de Pepino con Limon (Cucumber & Lime Water), 34

Agua Fresca de Piña Colada (Creamy Pineapple and Coconut Water), 38

Agua Fresca de Sandia y Pepino (Watermelon and Cucumber Water), 40

Anaheim peppers, 28

ancho peppers, 28

appetizers and sides, 54–73

  Arroz Blanco (White Rice), 65

  Arroz Rojo (Red Rice), 66

  Ceviche de Camarón (Shrimp Ceviche), 58

  Coctel de Camarón (Shrimp Cocktail), 60

  Ensalada de Calabacita (Mexican Squash and Avocado Salad), 56

  Ensalada de Pollo (Chicken Salad), 62

  Espagueti Rojo (Red Spaghetti), 70

  Espagueti Verde (Green Spaghetti), 68

  Frijoles de la Olla (Beans in a Pot), 64

  Tortitas de Papa y Queso (Cheesy Potato Cakes), 72

arbol peppers, 28

Arroz Blanco (White Rice), 65

Arroz con Leche (Rice Pudding), 216

Arroz con Pollo (Chicken and Rice), 170

Arroz Rojo (Red Rice), 66

Atole de Galletas (Creamy Cookie Atole), 50

Avocado Salsa (Salsa de Aguacate), 100

B

Baja Shrimp Tacos (Tacos de Camarón), 200

Barbacoa (Traditional Beef Barbacoa), 148

Barbacoa de Res (Chipotle Beef Barbacoa), 150

Basket Tacos (Tacos de Canasta), 194

bay leaves, 26

Bean Sauce Enchiladas (Enfrijoladas), 210

Beans in a Pot (Frijoles de la Olla), 64

Beef Birria (Birria de Res), 106

Beef Chili with Potatoes (Carne con Chiles y Papas), 116

beef entrees, 146–161

  Barbacoa (Traditional Beef Barbacoa), 148

  Barbacoa de Res (Chipotle Beef Barbacoa), 150

  Bistec Ranchero con Papas (Ranch Steak and Potatoes), 152

  Carne Asada (Marinated Steak), 156

  Discada, 158

  Gorditas de Picadillo en Chile Verde (Picadillo Stuffed Gorditas), 160

  Tacos de Deshebrada (Shredded Beef Tacos), 155

  Taquitos Dorados de Carne Molida (Ground Beef and Potato Taquitos), 154

Beer-Battered Fish Tacos (Tacos de Pescado), 204

Bionicos (Fruit and Cream Salad), 218

Bistec Ranchero con Papas (Ranch Steak and Potatoes), 152

bread and tortillas, 74–87

  Concha (Mexican Sweet Bread), 78

  Donas Mexicanas (Cinnamon Sugar Donuts), 82

  Masa Basica para Antojitos (Fried Masa), 80

  Masa para Tamales (Tamale Dough), 81

  Pan Bolillo (Mexican Rolls), 76

  Tortillas de Harina (Flour Tortillas), 84

  Tortillas de Maiz (Corn Tortillas), 86

Breakfast Burrito (Burritos para el Desayuno), 140

breakfast entrees, 134–145

  Burritos para el Desayuno (Breakfast Burrito), 140

  Chilaquiles Rojos (Red Chilaquiles), 136

  Chilaquiles Verde (Green Chilaquiles), 138

Huevos Ahogados (Drowned Eggs), 144

Huevos Encobijados (Eggs in a Blanket), 141

Huevos Rancheros (Mexican-Style Eggs), 142

broiler, method of roasting using, 31

Buñuelos (Mexican Fritters), 226

Burritos para el Desayuno (Breakfast Burrito), 140

C

Café de Olla (Spiced Coffee), 44

Café de Olla Helado (Iced Coffee), 42

Camarónes a la Diabla (Deviled Shrimp), 198

Carne Asada (Marinated Steak), 156

Carnitas (Slow-Cooked Pulled Pork), 186

Ceviche de Camarón (Shrimp Ceviche), 58

Champurrado (Chocolate Atole), 52

cheese. See quesos and creams

Cheesy Fajita Tacos (Tacos de Alambre), 174

Cheesy Potato Cakes (Tortitas de Papa y Queso), 72

Cheesy Shrimp Tacos (Tacos Gobernador), 202

chicken entrees, 162–181

Arroz con Pollo (Chicken and Rice), 170

Enchiladas Verdes con Pollo (Green Chicken Enchiladas), 164

Enmoladas con Pollo (Mole Sauce Enchiladas with Chicken), 166

Entomatadas con Pollo (Tomato Sauce Enchiladas with Chicken), 171

Mole de Pollo (Chicken Mole), 172

Pollo Asado (Marinated Grilled Chicken), 168

Tacos de Alambre (Cheesy Fajita Tacos), 174

Taquitos Dorados de Pollo con Consommé (Drowned Chicken Taquitos), 176

Tinga de Pollo (Chicken Tinga), 178

Tinga Verde de Pollo (Green Chicken Tinga), 180

Chicken Mole (Mole de Pollo), 172

Chicken and Rice (Arroz con Pollo), 170

Chicken and Rice Soup (Caldo de Pollo con Arroz), 112

Chicken Salad (Ensalada de Pollo), 62

Chicken Tinga (Tinga de Pollo), 178

Chicken and Tortilla Soup (Sopa Azteca), 132

Chilaquiles Rojos (Red Chilaquiles), 136

Chilaquiles Verde (Green Chilaquiles), 138

Chile con Queso Dip (Chili con Queso Dip), 101

Chile Rellenos (Stuffed Poblano Peppers), 206

Chili-Braised Pork (Chilorio), 188

Chili Colorado Tamales with Special Sauce (Tamales Rojos), 190

Chili con Queso Dip (Chile con Queso Dip), 101

Chilorio (Chili-Braised Pork), 188

Chipotle Beef Barbacoa (Barbacoa de Res), 150

chipotle peppers, 28

Choco Flan (Impossible Flan Cake), 228

Chocolate Atole (Champurrado), 52

Chocolate Horchata (Horchata de Chocolate), 48

Chorizo and Potato Sandwich (Pambazos de Papas con Chorizo), 192

Churros, 225

Cinnamon Sugar Donuts (Donas Mexicanas), 82

Coctel de Camarón (Shrimp Cocktail), 60

comal, 24

Concha (Mexican Sweet Bread), 78

concha cutter, 24

Corn Tortillas (Tortillas de Maiz), 86

creams and quesos, 27

crema Mexicana, 27

queso cotija, 27

queso fresco, 27

queso Oaxaca, 27

queso panela, 27

Creamy Cookie Atole (Atole de Galletas), 50

Creamy Pineapple and Coconut Water (Agua Fresca de Piña Colada), 38

crema Mexicana, 27

Cucumber & Lime Water (Agua Fresca de Pepino con Limon), 34

cumin, 26

D

desserts, 214–231

Arroz con Leche (Rice Pudding), 216

Bionicos (Fruit and Cream Salad), 218

Buñuelos (Mexican Fritters), 226

Choco Flan (Impossible Flan Cake), 228

Churros, 225

Fresca con Crema (Strawberries and Cream), 220

Gelatina de Mosaico (Mosaic Gelatin), 222

Gelatina Fresas con Crema (Strawberries and Cream Gelatin), 224

Pastel Tres Leches (3 Milk Cake), 230

Deviled Shrimp (Camarónes a la Diabla), 198

dips and salsas, 88–101

Chile con Queso Dip (Chili con Queso Dip), 101

Guacamole, 90

Pico de Gallo, 92

Salsa de Aguacate (Avocado Salsa), 100

Salsa Macha (Spicy Chile Oil Salsa), 94

Salsa Roja (Red Salsa), 96

Salsa Verde (Green Salsa), 98

Discada, 158

Donas Mexicanas (Cinnamon Sugar Donuts), 82

dried peppers, roasting, 31

drinks, 32–53

Agua Fresca de Hibisco con Fresas (Strawberry Hibiscus Water), 36

Agua Fresca de Pepino con Limon (Cucumber & Lime Water), 34

Agua Fresca de Piña Colada (Creamy Pineapple and Coconut Water), 38

Agua Fresca de Sandia y Pepino (Watermelon and Cucumber Water), 40

Atole de Galletas (Creamy Cookie Atole), 50

Café de Olla (Spiced Coffee), 44

Café de Olla Helado (Iced Coffee), 42

Champurrado (Chocolate Atole), 52

Horchata, 46

Horchata de Chocolate (Chocolate Horchata), 48

Horchata de Fresa (Strawberry Horchata), 45

Drowned Chicken Taquitos (Taquitos Dorados de Pollo con Consommé), 176

Drowned Eggs (Huevos Ahogados), 144

E

egg entries. See seafood, veggie and egg entrees

Eggs in a Blanket (Huevos Encobijados), 141

electric stove, method of roasting using, 31

Enchiladas Rojas (Red Enchiladas), 208

Enchiladas Verdes con Pollo (Green Chicken Enchiladas), 164

Enfrijoladas (Bean Sauce Enchiladas), 210

Enmoladas con Pollo (Mole Sauce Enchiladas with Chicken), 166

Ensalada de Calabacita (Mexican Squash and Avocado Salad), 56

Ensalada de Pollo (Chicken Salad), 62

Entomatadas con Pollo (Tomato Sauce Enchiladas with Chicken), 171

entrees

beef, 146–161

Barbacoa (Traditional Beef Barbacoa), 148

Barbacoa de Res (Chipotle Beef Barbacoa), 150

Bistec Ranchero con Papas (Ranch Steak and Potatoes), 152

Carne Asada (Marinated Steak), 156

Discada, 158

Gorditas de Picadillo en Chile Verde (Picadillo Stuffed Gorditas), 160

Tacos de Deshebrada (Shredded Beef Tacos), 155

Taquitos Dorados de Carne Molida (Ground Beef and Potato Taquitos), 154

breakfast, 134–145

Burritos para el Desayuno (Breakfast Burrito), 140

Chilaquiles Rojos (Red Chilaquiles), 136

Chilaquiles Verde (Green Chilaquiles), 138

Huevos Ahogados (Drowned Eggs), 144

Huevos Encobijados (Eggs in a Blanket), 141

Huevos Rancheros (Mexican-Style Eggs), 142

chicken, 162–181

Arroz con Pollo (Chicken and Rice), 170

Enchiladas Verdes con Pollo (Green Chicken Enchiladas), 164

Enmoladas con Pollo (Mole Sauce Enchiladas with Chicken), 166

Entomatadas con Pollo (Tomato Sauce Enchiladas with Chicken), 171

Mole de Pollo (Chicken Mole), 172

Pollo Asado (Marinated Grilled Chicken), 168

Tacos de Alambre (Cheesy Fajita Tacos), 174

Taquitos Dorados de Pollo con Consome (Drowned Chicken Taquitos), 176

Tinga de Pollo (Chicken Tinga), 178

Tinga Verde de Pollo (Green Chicken Tinga), 180

pork, 182–195

Carnitas (Slow-Cooked Pulled Pork), 186

Chilorio (Chili-Braised Pork), 188

Pambazos de Papas con Chorizo (Chorizo and Potato Sandwich), 192

Tacos de Canasta (Basket Tacos), 194

Tacos al Pastor (Shepherd-Style Tacos), 184

Tamales Rojos (Chili Colorado Tamales with Special Sauce), 190

Tamales Verde (Green Pork Tamales), 189

seafood, veggie and egg entrees, 196–213

Camarónes a la Diabla (Deviled Shrimp), 198

Chile Rellenos (Stuffed Poblano Peppers), 206

Enchiladas Rojas (Red Enchiladas), 208

Enfrijoladas (Bean Sauce Enchiladas), 210

Migas a la Mexicana (Mexican-Style Scrambled Eggs and Chips), 212

Tacos de Camarón (Baja Shrimp Tacos), 200

Tacos Gobernador (Cheesy Shrimp Tacos), 202

Tacos de Pescado (Beer-Battered Fish Tacos), 204

Tamales de Rajas con Queso (Poblano Rajas and Cheese Tamales), 205

equipment, 24

comal, 24

concha cutter, 24

molcajete, 24
molinillo, 24
tortilla press, 24
tortilla warmer, 24
Espagueti Rojo (Red Spaghetti), 70
Espagueti Verde (Green Spaghetti), 68

F

Flour Tortillas (Tortillas de Harina), 84
Fresca con Crema (Strawberries and
  Cream), 220
Fried Masa (Masa Basica para
  Antojitos), 80
Frijoles de la Olla (Beans in a Pot), 64
Fruit and Cream Salad (Bionicos), 218

G

gas stove, method of roasting
  using, 31
Gelatina de Mosaico (Mosaic
  Gelatin), 222
Gelatina Fresas con Crema
  (Strawberries and Cream
  Gelatin), 224
Gorditas de Picadillo en Chile Verde
  (Picadillo Stuffed Gorditas), 160
Green Chicken Enchiladas (Enchiladas
  Verdes con Pollo), 164
Green Chicken Soup (Pozole Verde de
  Pollo), 124
Green Chicken Tinga (Tinga Verde de
  Pollo), 180
Green Chilaquiles (Chilaquiles
  Verde), 138
green peppers, roasting, 31
Green Pork Tamales (Tamales
  Verde), 189
Green Salsa (Salsa Verde), 98
Green Spaghetti (Espagueti Verde), 68
Ground Beef and Potato Taquitos
  (Taquitos Dorados de Carne
  Molida), 154
Guacamole, 90
guajillo peppers, 28

H

Hearty Beef and Vegetable Soup
  (Caldo de Res), 114
Hearty Beef and Vegetable Soup in
  Guajillo Sauce (Mole de Olla), 126
herbs, spices and others, 26
  bay leaves, 26
  cumin, 26
  Mexican chocolate, 26
  Mexican oregano, 26
  piloncillo, 26
  whole cloves, 26
Horchata, 46
Horchata de Chocolate (Chocolate
  Horchata), 48
Horchata de Fresca (Strawberry
  Horchata), 45
Huevos Ahogados (Drowned
  Eggs), 144
Huevos Encobijados (Eggs in a
  Blanket), 141
Huevos Rancheros (Mexican-Style
  Eggs), 142

I–J

Iced Coffee (Café de Olla Helado), 42
Impossible Flan Cake (Choco
  Flan), 228
ingredients, 26–28
  herbs, spices and others, 26
  peppers and tomatillos, 28   quesos
    and creams, 27

K–L

kitchen essentials, 22–31
  equipment, 24
    comal, 24
    concha cutter, 24
    molcajete, 24
    molinillo, 24
    tortilla press, 24
    tortilla warmer, 24
  ingredients, 26–28
  roasting steps and techniques, 31

M

Marinated Grilled Chicken (Pollo
  Asado), 168
Marinated Steak (Carne Asada), 156
Masa Basica para Antojitos (Fried
  Masa), 80
Masa para Tamales (Tamale
  Dough), 81
Meatball Soup (Caldo de
  Albóndigas), 108
Mexican chocolate, 26
Mexican Fritters (Buñuelos), 226
Mexican oregano, 26
Mexican Rolls (Pan Bolillo), 76
Mexican Squash and Avocado Salad
  (Ensalada de Calabacita), 56
Mexican-Style Eggs (Huevos
  Rancheros), 142
Mexican-Style Scrambled Eggs and
  Chips (Migas a la Mexicana), 212
Mexican Sweet Bread (Concha), 78
Migas a la Mexicana (Mexican-Style
  Scrambled Eggs and Chips), 212
molcajete, 24
Mole de Pollo (Chicken Mole), 172
Mole Sauce Enchiladas with Chicken
  (Enmoladas con Pollo), 166
molinillo, 24
Mosaic Gelatin (Gelatina de
  Mosaico), 222

N–O–P

New Mexico peppers, 28

Pambazos de Papas con Chorizo
  (Chorizo and Potato Sandwich), 192
Pan Bolillo (Mexican Rolls), 76
Pastel Tres Leches (3 Milk Cake), 230
peppers, roasting, 31
peppers and tomatillos, 28
  Anaheim peppers, 28
  ancho peppers, 28
  arbol peppers, 28
  chipotle peppers, 28
  guajillo peppers, 28
  New Mexico peppers, 28
  poblano peppers, 28

serrano peppers, 28

tomatillos, 28

Picadillo Stuffed Gorditas (Gorditas de Picadillo en Chile Verde), 160

Pico de Gallo, 92

piloncillo, 26

poblano peppers, 28

Poblano Rajas and Cheese Tamales (Tamales de Rajas con Queso), 205

Pollo Asado (Marinated Grilled Chicken), 168

pork entrees, 182–195

Carnitas (Slow-Cooked Pulled Pork), 186

Chilorio (Chili-Braised Pork), 188

Pambazos de Papas con Chorizo (Chorizo and Potato Sandwich), 192

Tacos de Canasta (Basket Tacos), 194

Tacos al Pastor (Shepherd-Style Tacos), 184

Tamales Rojos (Chili Colorado Tamales with Special Sauce), 190

Tamales Verdes (Green Pork Tamales), 189

Q

quesos and creams, 27

crema Mexicana, 27

queso cotija, 27

queso fresco, 27

queso Oaxaca, 27

queso panela, 27

R

Ranch Steak and Potatoes (Bistec Ranchero con Papas), 152

Red Beef Chili (Chile Colorado), 118

Red Chilaquiles (Chilaquiles Rojos), 136

Red Enchiladas (Enchiladas Rojas), 208

Red Pepper Tripe Stew (Menudo), 122

Red Pork Chili (Asado de Boda), 104

Red Pork Soup (Pozole Rojo), 128

Red Rice (Arroz Rojo), 66

Red Salsa (Salsa Roja), 96

Red Spaghetti (Espagueti Rojo), 70

Regalado family, 20–21

Rice Pudding (Arroz con Leche), 216

roasting steps and techniques, 31

broiler, 31

dried peppers, 31

electric stove, 31

gas stove, 31

green peppers, 31

spices, 31

tomatillos, 31

tomatoes, 31

S

salsas, dips and, 88–101

Chile con Queso Dip (Chili con Queso Dip), 101

Guacamole, 90

Pico de Gallo, 92

Salsa de Aguacate (Avocado Salsa), 100

Salsa Macha (Spicy Chile Oil Salsa), 94

Salsa Roja (Red Salsa), 96

Salsa Verde (Green Salsa), 98

seafood, veggie and egg entrees, 196–213

Camarónes a la Diabla (Deviled Shrimp), 198

Chile Rellenos (Stuffed Poblano Peppers), 206

Enchiladas Rojas (Red Enchiladas), 208

Enfrijoladas (Bean Sauce Enchiladas), 210

Migas a la Mexicana (Mexican-Style Scrambled Eggs and Chips), 212

Tacos de Camarón (Baja Shrimp Tacos), 200

Tacos Gobernador (Cheesy Shrimp Tacos), 202

Tacos de Pescado (Beer-Battered Fish Tacos), 204

Tamales de Rajas con Queso (Poblano Rajas and Cheese Tamales), 205

serrano peppers, 28

Shell and Chicken Soup (Sopa de Conchitas con Pollo), 117

Shepherd-Style Tacos (Tacos al Pastor), 184

Shredded Beef Tacos (Tacos de Deshebrada), 155

Shrimp Ceviche (Ceviche de Camarón), 58

Shrimp Cocktail (Coctel de Camarón), 60

Shrimp Soup (Caldo de Camarón), 110

sides and appetizers, 54–73

Arroz Blanco (White Rice), 65

Arroz Rojo (Red Rice), 66

Ceviche de Camarón (Shrimp Ceviche), 58

Coctel de Camarón (Shrimp Cocktail), 60

Ensalada de Calabacita (Mexican Squash and Avocado Salad), 56

Ensalada de Pollo (Chicken Salad), 62

Espagueti Rojo (Red Spaghetti), 70

Espagueti Verde (Green Spaghetti), 68

Frijoles de la Olla (Beans in a Pot), 64

Tortitas de Papa y Queso (Cheesy Potato Cakes), 72

Slow Cooked Green Chili (Chile Verde), 120

Slow-Cooked Pulled Pork (Carnitas), 186

soups and stews, 102–133

Asado de Boda (Red Pork Chili), 104

Birria de Res (Beef Birria), 106

Caldo de Albóndigas (Meatball Soup), 108

Caldo de Camarón (Shrimp Soup), 110

Caldo de Pollo con Arroz (Chicken and Rice Soup), 112

Caldo de Res (Hearty Beef and Vegetable Soup), 114

Carne con Chiles y Papas (Beef Chili with Potatoes), 116

Chile Colorado (Red Beef Chili), 118

Chile Verde (Slow Cooked Green Chili), 120

Menudo (Red Pepper Tripe Stew), 122

Mole de Olla (Hearty Beef and Vegetable Soup in Guajillo Sauce), 126

Pozole Rojo (Red Pork Soup), 128

Pozole Verde de Pollo (Green Chicken Soup), 124

Sopa Azteca (Chicken and Tortilla Soup), 132

Sopa de Conchitas con Pollo (Shell and Chicken Soup), 117

Sopa de Fideo con Carne (Vermicelli Soup with Beef and Potatoes), 130

Spiced Coffee (Café de Olla), 44

spices, roasting, 31. *See also* herbs, spices and others

Spicy Chile Oil Salsa (Salsa Macha), 94

stews and soups, 102–133

Asado de Boda (Red Pork Chili), 104

Birria de Res (Beef Birria), 106

Caldo de Albóndigas (Meatball Soup), 108

Caldo de Camarón (Shrimp Soup), 110

Caldo de Pollo con Arroz (Chicken and Rice Soup), 112

Caldo de Res (Hearty Beef and Vegetable Soup), 114

Carne con Chiles y Papas (Beef Chili with Potatoes), 116

Chile Colorado (Red Beef Chili), 118

Chile Verde (Slow Cooked Green Chili), 120

Menudo (Red Pepper Tripe Stew), 122

Mole de Olla (Hearty Beef and Vegetable Soup in Guajillo Sauce), 126

Pozole Rojo (Red Pork Soup), 128

Pozole Verde de Pollo (Green Chicken Soup), 124

Sopa Azteca (Chicken and Tortilla Soup), 132

Sopa de Conchitas con Pollo (Shell and Chicken Soup), 117

Sopa de Fideo con Carne (Vermicelli Soup with Beef and Potatoes), 130

Strawberries and Cream (Fresca con Crema), 220

Strawberries and Cream Gelatin (Gelatina Fresas con Crema), 224

Strawberry Hibiscus Water (Agua Fresca de Jamaica con Fresas), 36

Strawberry Horchata (Horchata de Fresca), 45

Stuffed Poblano Peppers (Chile Rellenos), 206

T–U–V

Tacos de Alambre (Cheesy Fajita Tacos), 174

Tacos de Camarón (Baja Shrimp Tacos), 200

Tacos de Canasta (Basket Tacos), 194

Tacos de Deshebrada (Shredded Beef Tacos), 155

Tacos Gobernador (Cheesy Shrimp Tacos), 202

Tacos al Pastor (Shepherd-Style Tacos), 184

Tacos de Pescado (Beer-Battered Fish Tacos), 204

Tamale Dough (Masa para Tamales), 81

Tamales de Rajas con Queso (Poblano Rajas and Cheese Tamales), 205

Tamales Rojos (Chili Colorado Tamales with Special Sauce), 190

Tamales Verdes (Green Pork Tamales), 189

Taquitos Dorados de Carne Molida (Ground Beef and Potato Taquitos), 154

Taquitos Dorados de Pollo con Consome (Drowned Chicken Taquitos), 176

3 Milk Cake (Pastel Tres Leches), 230

Tinga de Pollo (Chicken Tinga), 178

Tinga Verde de Pollo (Green Chicken Tinga), 180

tomatillos, 28, 31

tomatoes, roasting, 31

Tomato Sauce Enchiladas with Chicken (Entomatadas con Pollo), 171

tortilla press, 24

tortillas and bread, 74–87

Concha (Mexican Sweet Bread), 78

Donas Mexicanas (Cinnamon Sugar Donuts), 82

Masa Basica para Antojitos (Fried Masa), 80

Masa para Tamales (Tamale Dough), 81

Pan Bolillo (Mexican Rolls), 76

Tortillas de Harina (Flour Tortillas), 84

Tortillas de Maiz (Corn Tortillas), 86

Tortillas de Harina (Flour Tortillas), 84

Tortillas de Maiz (Corn Tortillas), 86

tortilla warmer, 24

Tortitas de Papa y Queso (Cheesy Potato Cakes), 72

Traditional Beef Barbacoa (Barbacoa), 148

veggie entrees. *See* seafood, veggie and egg entrees

Vermicelli Soup with Beef and Potatoes (Sopa de Fideo con Carne), 130

W–X–Y–Z

Watermelon and Cucumber Water (Agua Fresca de Sandia y Pepino), 40

White Rice (Arroz Blanco), 65

whole cloves, 26

Acknowledgments

To my mom, for getting me in the kitchen and making me responsible at such an early age. Not only did you prepare me for marriage but also for what was coming my way in life. And to my dad, for never leaving my side and always reminding me to work hard for everthing I want in life. I hope I made you proud, *amá y apá!*

To my kids, Angel, Nathaniel, Natalie, Jayden, and Gio. I hope you're proud of Mom because regardless of all the hardships we've gone through, we did it! I've shown you how to keep going, never stop believing in yourself, and how to do it all with love and a big smile on your face! The sky isn't the limit—the mind is. So keep shining, my loves. Thank you for being my #1 fans and for being my motivation every single day.

To my husband, Lewis, for pushing me every day, encouraging and supporting me, being with me every step of the way, being the best cameraman, and, most important of all, being my person and the one I can always count on.

To my editor, Brandon, and the entire DK and Penguin Random House team, for the opportunity, guidance, and faith in me and in this book.

And to my YouTube family, for believing in me and my recipes, making all of this possible.

About the Author

Claudia Regalado is a content creator focusing on cooking authentic Mexican cuisine. Watching and learning from her mother and grandmother as a child, Claudia has since honed her cooking skills preparing meals for her family and friends for years. Her YouTube channel, Cooking con Claudia, has entertained millions with her videos spanning all aspects of Mexican cooking.

And now for the best part!